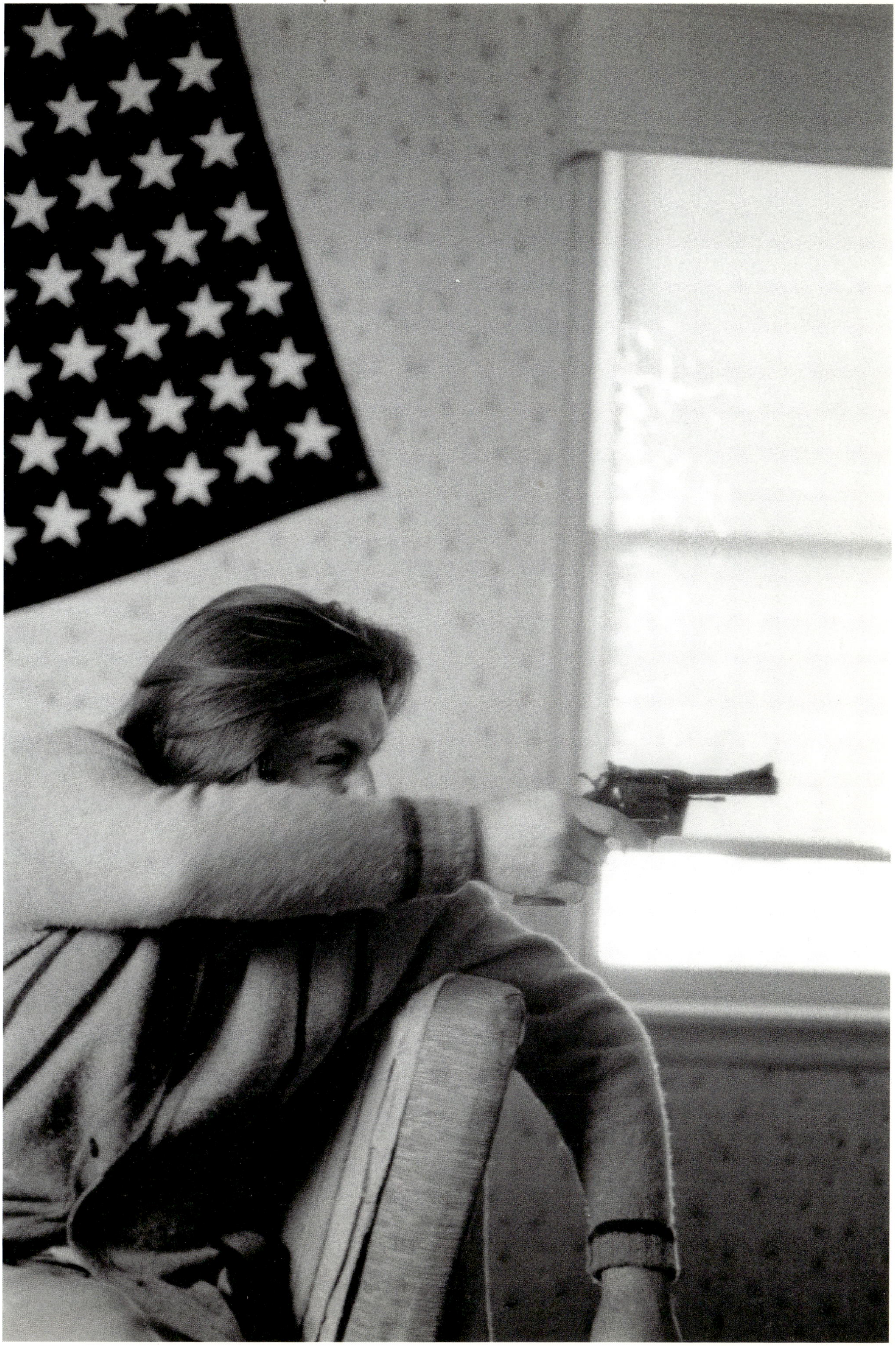

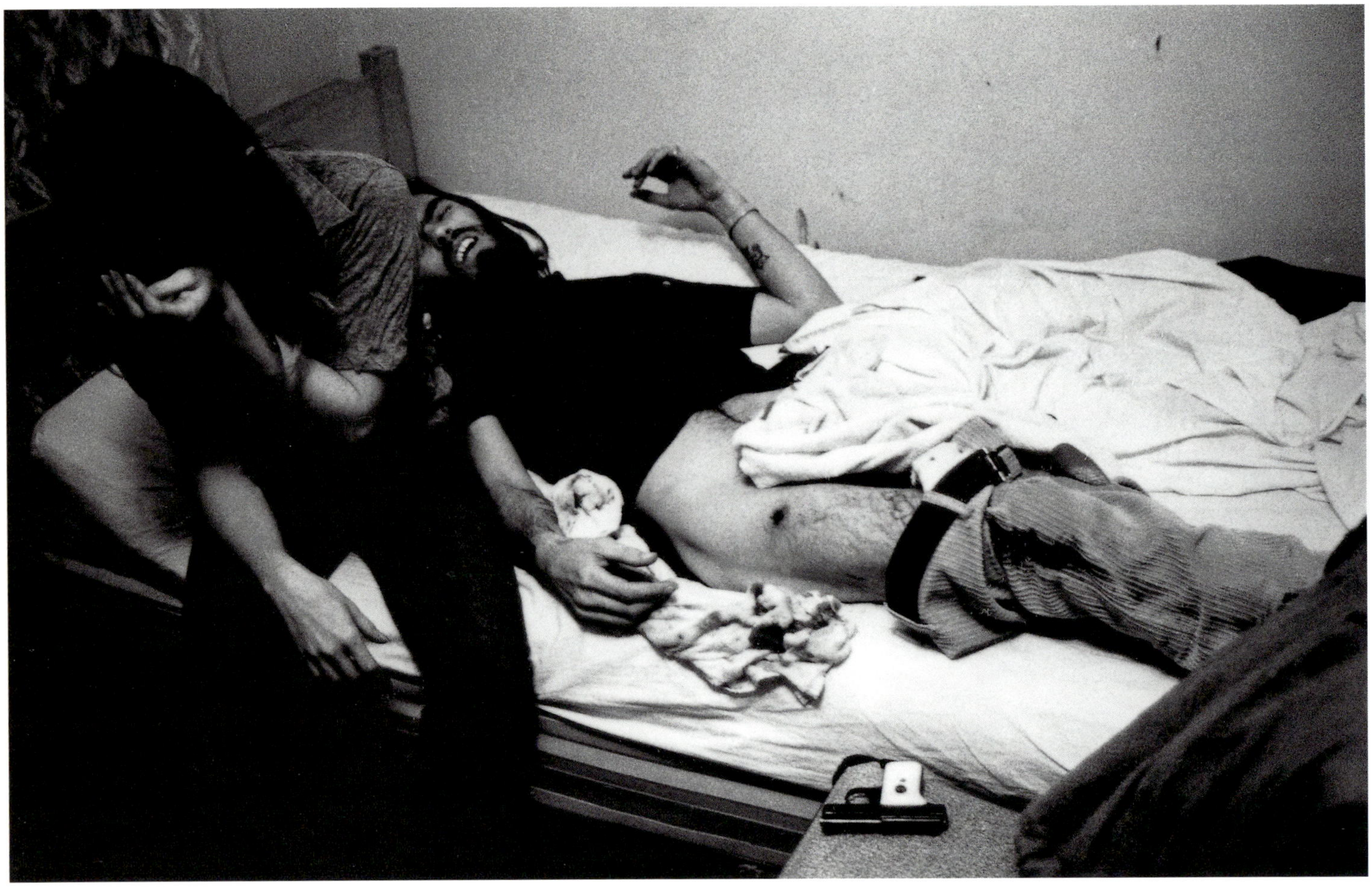

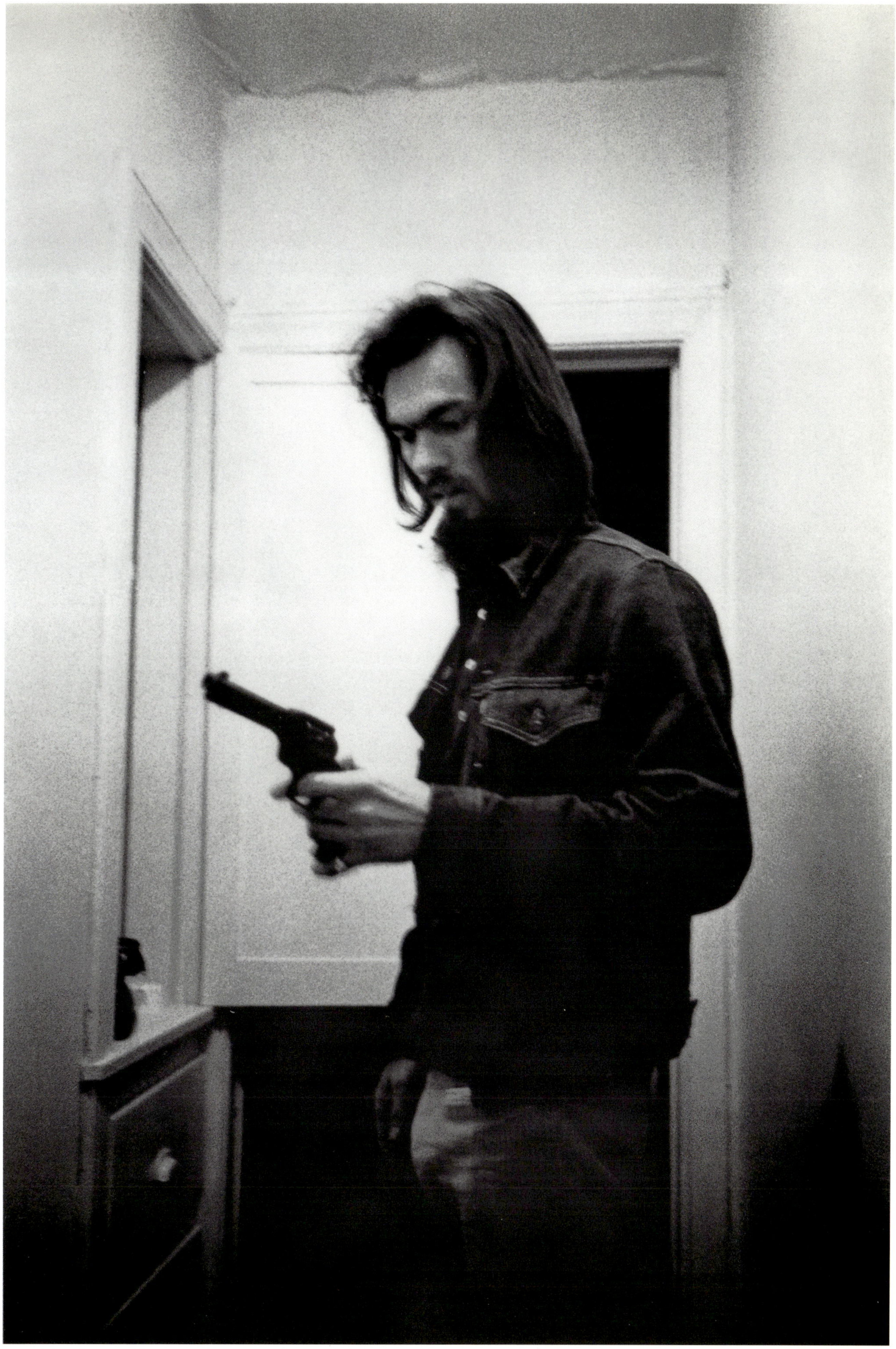

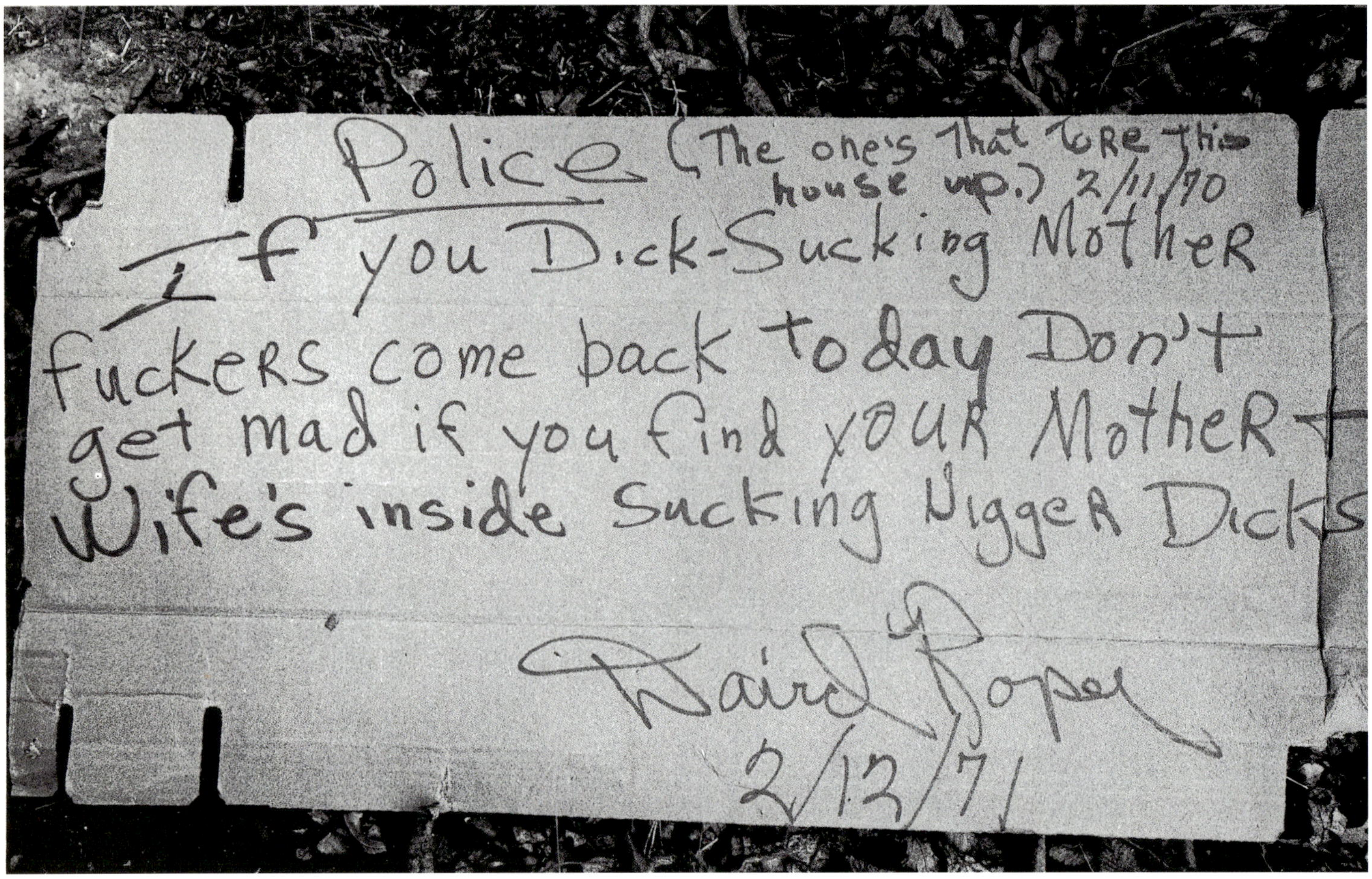
Police (The one's That Tore This house up.) 2/11/70
If you Dick-Sucking Mother
fuckers come back today Don't
get mad if you find YOUR Mother +
Wife's inside Sucking Nigger Dicks
David Roper
2/13/71

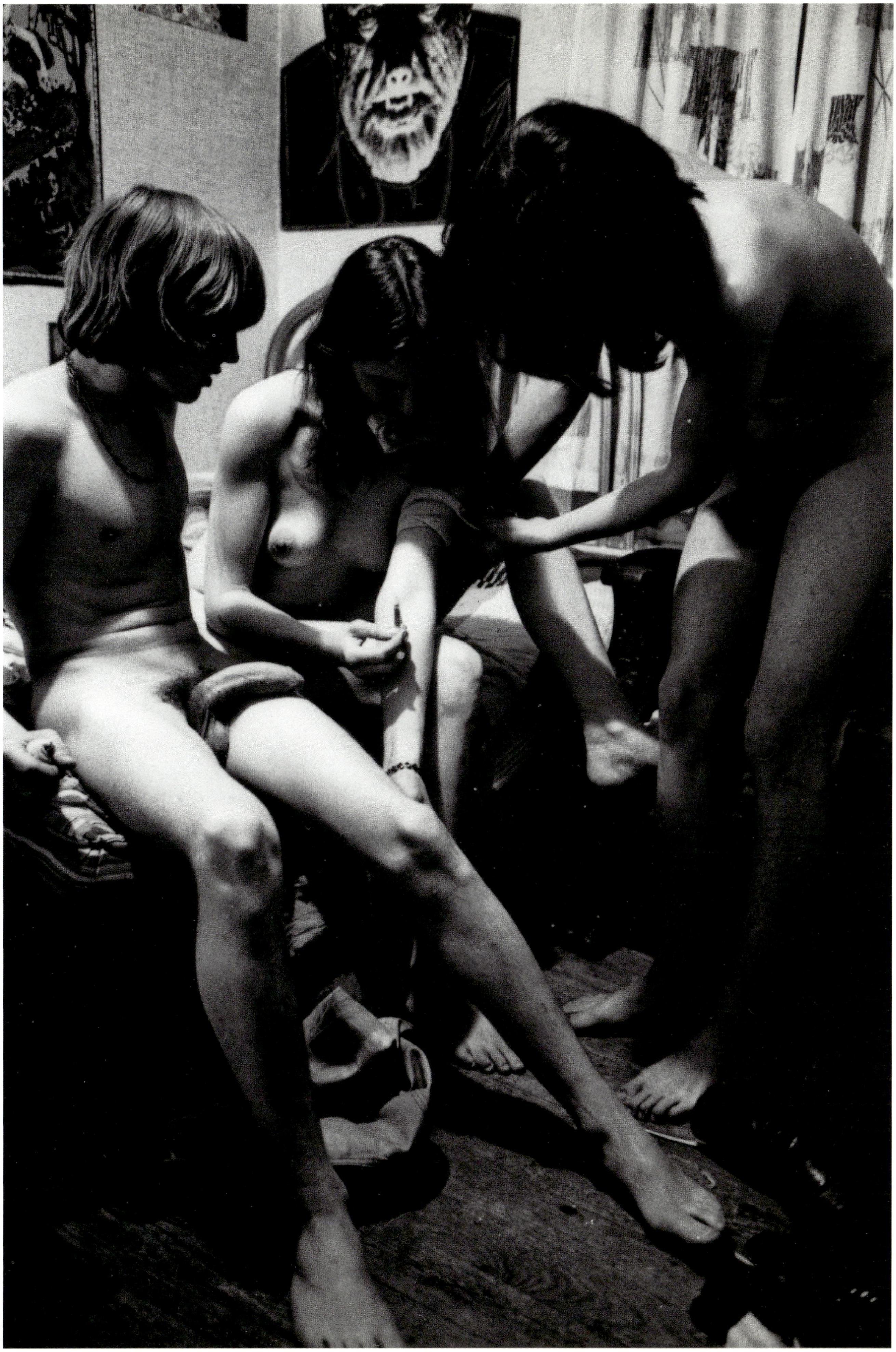

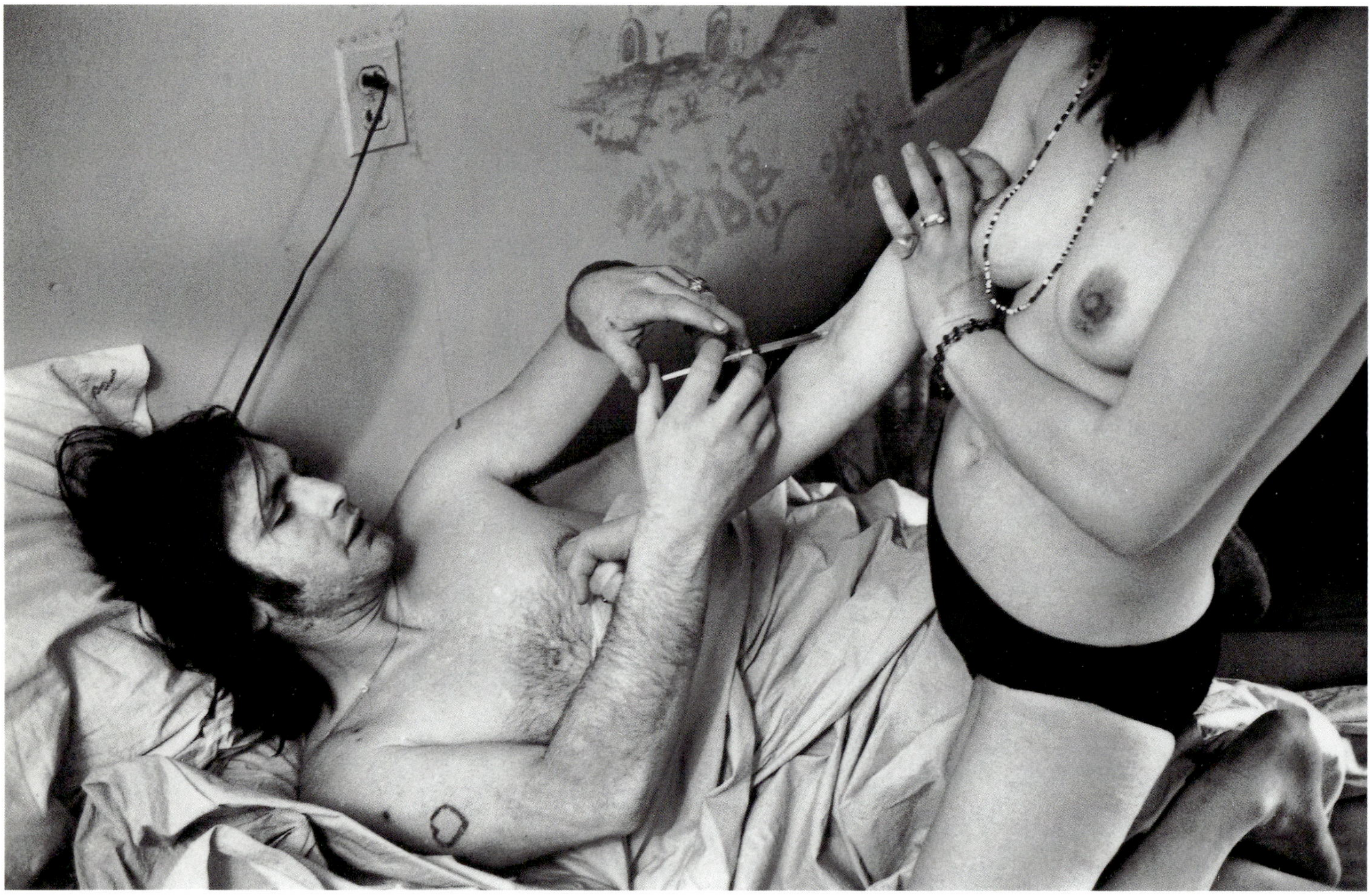

Philip Monk

The American Trip

Larry Clark, Nan Goldin, Cady Noland, Richard Prince

2 February – 8 April 1996

The Power Plant
Contemporary Art Gallery at Harbourfront Centre

231 Queens Quay West
Toronto, Ontario
Canada M5J 2G8
(416) 973-4949

Canadian Cataloguing in Publication Data

Monk, Philip, 1950–
The American trip: Larry Clark, Nan Goldin, Cady Noland, Richard Prince

Catalogue of an exhibition held at The Power Plant–Contemporary Art Gallery at Harbourfront Centre, Feb. 2–Apr. 8, 1996.
ISBN 0-921047-07-X

1. Photography – United States – Exhibitions.
2. Photography, Artistic – Exhibitions. I. Power Plant (Art Gallery). II. Title.

TR644.M65 1996 770'.0973'074713541 C95–933079–8

PAGES 1–6
Larry Clark
Tulsa 1971

The Girl Next Door

the girl next door

—caption of a photograph in Larry Clark's *Teenage Lust*

The biker chicks *are* the girls next door.

—Richard Prince

Hi Girl!

—chapter title on New York drag queens from *The Other Side* by Nan Goldin

This is how I want a killer kid to look, like the kid next door.

—Larry Clark

Some of American art's most compelling images originate in the margins. The rich tradition of social documentary in American photography from Jacob Riis and Lewis Hine to Walker Evans and the FSA photographers documented the poor and disenfranchised in cities and countryside. Not having chosen their position, the disenfranchised were doubly marginalized, first economically and then in images that indicted society for its inequities. Delegates of mainstream society, the photographers were on the outside looking in, and their subjects—why expect otherwise—had no means of self-representation. It was not until past mid-century, notably with Robert Frank in the 1950s and Diane Arbus in the 1960s, that photography loosened its editorializing grip and social function was displaced to personal statement, however ambivalent that intention might have been. While still picturing the social milieu—but by shifting its subjects—and not rejecting it in favour of the purely pictorial, these photographers uncovered views of America hitherto not memorialized but now widely recognized as classic expressions of the period. (Moral purpose was still built into the critical response, which usually focused on something not quite American to the reviewer.) Frank's mode of representation was centrifugal, and his restless criss-cross of America corresponded to the Beats' road trips; Arbus's was centripetal in her discovery of the outsider, the "freak," within society, a "voyeurism" that aligned her to Andy Warhol. These means of getting images brought these photographers into a different lived experience with their subjects. This identification, combined with their diverse modes of artistic practice, are the parameters within which the artists in this exhibition articulate their work.

The impulse towards the margins, its values and experiences, first as a geographic expression in the late-nineteenth-century drift to the West, then as an internal element of society starting in the late 1940s and 1950s with, among others, the Beats' rejection of the postwar American middle-class ethos, is well known. What is less documented is the role artists have played in portraying subcultures for a wider public, as well as the complex intermingling and communication between artists' and the mainstream's depictions of the outsider.

The American Trip looks at the continuing fascination of artists with the margins of American society. The exhibition is devoted to the persistence of the "theme of the outlaw" in the works of the contemporary artists Larry Clark, Nan Goldin, Cady Noland, and Richard Prince. These artists have created durable images of various outsider scenes in one of two ways. They have meditated on iconic images of outlawhood, in the cases of Noland and Prince by using images that already dwell in the public realm to different degrees of visibility and cultural resonance. (Noland, for instance, uses wire-service photographs of Lee Harvey Oswald, the Manson family, and Patty Hearst, among others; Prince rephotographs images from a variety of subculture speciality magazines—*Outlaw Biker*, to take a representative example.) Or the artists have been active participants in the various "outlaw" scenes they have photographed. (The early work of Larry Clark collected in *Tulsa* showed his home-town milieu of petty crime and drugs. He himself spent time in jail during what he calls his "outlaw years." Nan Goldin lived among the drag queens she has photographed as if they were an extended family, first in Boston in the early 1970s when they were still reviled—even in the gay community—and later in New York where they are now cultural heroes.) Prince and Noland exorcise and reinvest fascination with the iconic power of the image; Clark and Goldin bring to light new communities through the image.

Artists have always been at the forefront of the expression of "outlaw" activity. Sometimes they document it; sometimes they are involved in its creation. They represent outlaw culture and produce a "drifter" aesthetic. As the margins have migrated more and more to the interior of society through various forms of disillusion with the American Dream and rejection of its premises, artists have been first on the scene to give artistic rather than journalistic or sociological expression. As subcultures have become more diverse and their adherents younger and younger, the media have taken on a greater role in the dissemination of their attitudes and styles, especially when these subcultures lend themselves to commodification. But wherever we find a censorship issue, whenever we are on the edge of what can be said or not said, shown or not shown by artists, we have located the margin of an activity that society does not yet tolerate and must separate out and demonize by creating a boundary between inside and outside, between what it tolerates and what it considers beyond the pale.

Artists have been instrumental in pushing such boundaries and in normalizing the image of the outsider for public consumption. They reveal, record, and define. They give representational expression to a community and offer outsiders models of identification. Some might instead call this "popularizing" or even "romanticizing" that image. "Mainstreaming deviancy" is the way U.S. Senator Robert Dole, in a speech in Los Angeles in the summer of 1995, described it as he condemned the American entertainment industry for its glorification of sex and violence. Senator Dole is right . . . and wrong. He is correct when he speaks of one mood in American society, but he is wrong in suggesting that this is anything other than the American way, or what we expect it to be, as it has been championed during our long years of exposure to American myth through Hollywood film.

One of the films Dole singled out, Oliver Stone's media and tabloid satire *Natural Born Killers*, belongs to a particularly telling genre of Hollywood film and American myth—that of young lovers on a killing spree. Originating in the Depression with Warner Brothers gangster films, the celebration of kids becoming outlaws was later to recur in the French New Wave, imported in Hollywood films, and during the anti-authoritarian, youth-culture 1960s it resurfaced in American films such as *Bonnie and Clyde*. The Depression era was tolerant of the outlaw myth-in-the-making when ordinary people, kids often, became outlaws. In a new repression era, the *line* between inside and outside must clearly be drawn. That which we do not tolerate, we must place beyond the law. "A line has been crossed—not just of taste, but of human dignity and decency. It is crossed every time sexual violence is given a catchy tune. When teen suicide is set to an appealing beat. When Hollywood's dream factories turn out nightmares of depravity," said Dole. Society as much as individual choice determines what is the law and what is outside the law—and thus who is the out-law.

Hollywood alone cannot manufacture deviance; it must answer a need. "Popular culture never lies," Jay Landesman said. "Not about the people who consume it."[1] Society's horror is the shock of recognition of deviance within—the knowledge that the outlaw actually lives within us and the family may be its breeding ground. The role media play, in fact, is integral to the needs of society. Moreso than the law, they provide the vehicle by which individual members are elevated or degraded, celebrated or reviled. As

America's becomes increasingly a tabloid culture, these needs are circulated more rapidly. In fact, they must be identified and outstripped more quickly, and television confession shows now play a principal role in this process. Here production is linked to consumption, the quest for profit linked to the quest for ratings, ratings linked to an audience whose needs are thereby fulfilled. Depravity, it seems, is intimately, and scandalously, linked to capitalist profit.

The outlaw has a central place and necessary function in this dynamic process, which is, moreover, a two-way passage. One can pass from being an outlaw to being a celebrity as easily as from celebrity to outcast. In America, even every drifter has the potential to break into popular consciousness. And every celebrity is a target for tabloid smears. Sometimes the outlaw becomes renowned through his, usually violent, act upon a celebrity. Lee Harvey Oswald assassinating John Kennedy and Charles Manson responsible for the killing of Sharon Tate are two emblematic examples. Sometimes the two become one, as in the case of Patty Hearst, the celebrity (at least in name) who becomes an outlaw: the celebrity outlaw. In American society, the outlaw and celebrity are deeply connected. The outlaw exerts a fascination even when he or she is demonized as an outcast. From outlaw to celebrity and from Puritan stocks to tabloid exposure is not far.

If celebrity is then a result of the romance with the outlaw, celebrating heterodoxy is a consequence of bringing the margins to representation. Sometimes this occurs through the persona of an artist alone, when his or her celebrity draws attention to new personalities gathered into non-traditional communities. Warhol is *the* historical example, a new type of artistic personage around whom various subcultures coalesced. "From 1960 to 1968, the silver-covered other world of Warhol's loft on East Forty-seventh Street functioned as the place where the interlocking subcultures of the late 1950s—artistic, sexual, sometimes even criminal—were able at last to surface into the bright glamour of the 1960s affluent chic."[2] Paradoxically, focus on individual celebrity brings a wider community into the picture. (As erstwhile photographer to Warhol and his Factory, Richard Avedon is a complementary figure, a photographer able to move between the extremes of the elevated and the degraded, documenting the celebrated and reviled in his work. He produced some of the most excoriating images of defeat in his series of drifters from *In the American West*, where we find subjects beyond the limits of identification. Partly through the mechanisms of fashion, partly through his own fame, his work confers celebrity status.)

Nan Goldin's photographs reveal a different record of artists' own outlawed communities. Her subjects have taken longer to enter the mainstream, but they inhabit it fully now, with parades, films, and academic and glossy books devoted to drag queens. Goldin herself is celebrated in the pages of fashion magazines such as *Vogue*. Fashion photography, in a swing from the earlier upper-class fetishism of Helmut Newton to white-trash indecorum, now features exactly the sorts of scenes depicted in Goldin's or Clark's books. Clark's fashion influence is noted most recently in Calvin Klein's withdrawn summer 1995 advertising campaign, which coincided with the release of Clark's film *Kids*.

The dialogue between mainstream and margin is a subtheme of the exhibition, signalled especially in the persistent exchange between Hollywood and artists. Hollywood not only purveys and affects; it borrows and steals. While Warhol in the 1960s was making paintings of silkscreened images of 1950s Hollywood Method actors such as Marlon Brando in *The Wild One* and stars such as Marilyn Monroe and Elizabeth Taylor, he was directing his own superstars in films that were camp parodies of both Method acting and the Hollywood star system and a celebration of his own Factory demimonde. Kenneth Anger's classic 1963 underground film *Scorpio Rising* ironically documents the symbiotic relationship between media icons of delinquency—its stars Marlon

Brando and James Dean—and actual delinquent subcultures. In turn, his film influenced a whole series of exploitation biker films, starting with Roger Corman's *Wild Angels* and ending with Dennis Hopper's *Easy Rider*. The dialogue continues in Larry Clark's acknowledged impact on Gus Van Sant's *Drugstore Cowboy*, for instance, and Clark's own 1995 feature film *Kids*.

Celebrity and delinquency are bound together by the threat of corruption found in both Hollywood Babylon and teen babylonians. What starts as a celebration by artists is appropriated by the mainstream media and ends as panic in the press. Nowhere is the fear greater than in the heart of the American family, the locus of the worry, the terror even, that the enemy is within. In the same way that 1950s monster and sci-fi movies were sometimes read as worries over the "threat" of communism, so the worry now is that the kids are not "alright." The images of people in this exhibition show them not to be traditional outlaws. They are, as these artists celebrate, the girl—or boy—next door.

Notes

1 John Clellon Holmes, *Representative Men: The Biographical Essays* (Fayettesville: The University of Arkansas Press, 1988), 56.

2 Stephen Koch, *Star-Gazer: Andy Warhol's World and His Films* (New York: Praeger, 1973), 3.

PAGES 13–14
Larry Clark
Untitled ("Forty-second Street Series") 1979
Untitled ("Forty-second Street Series") 1984

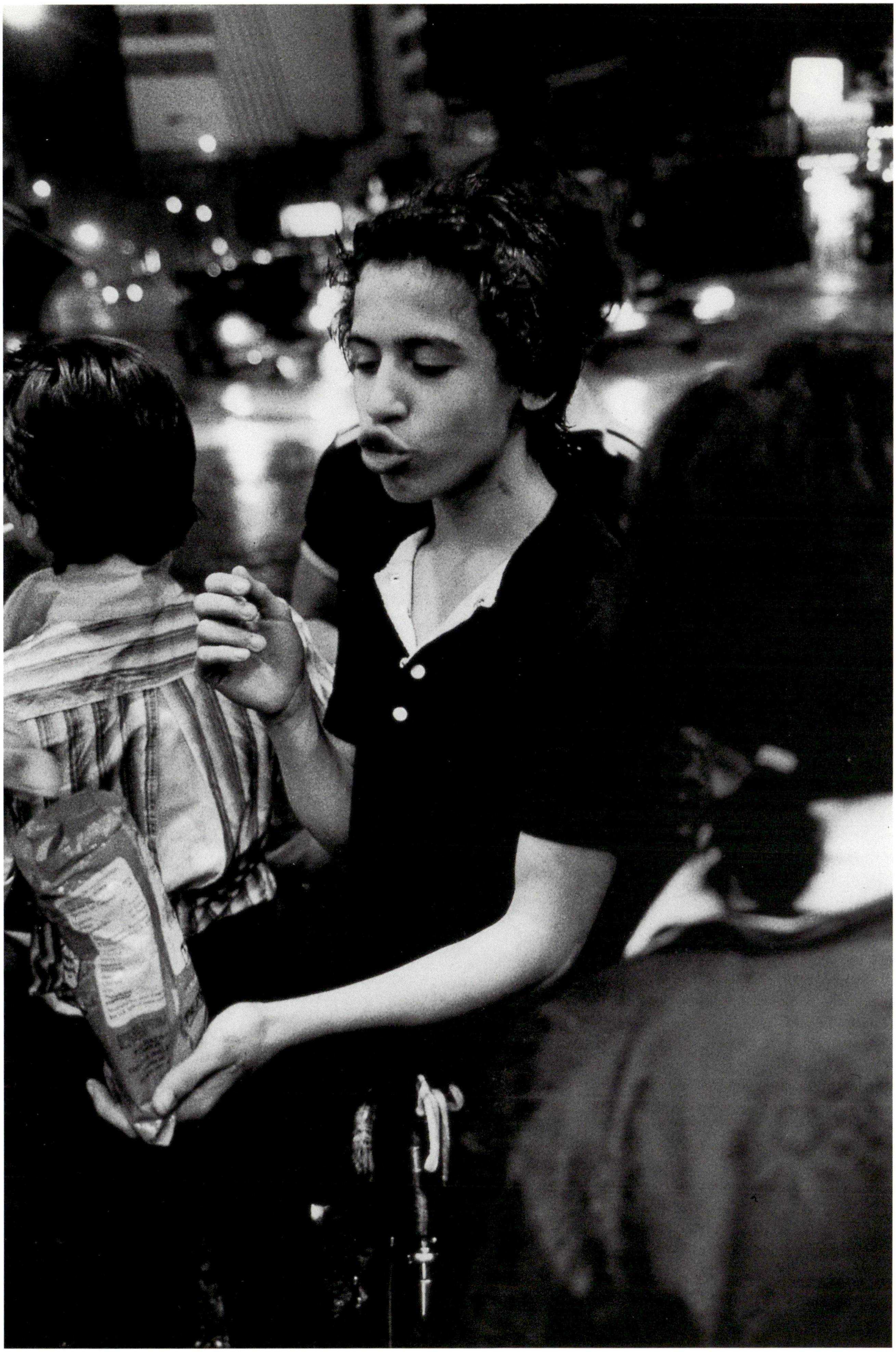

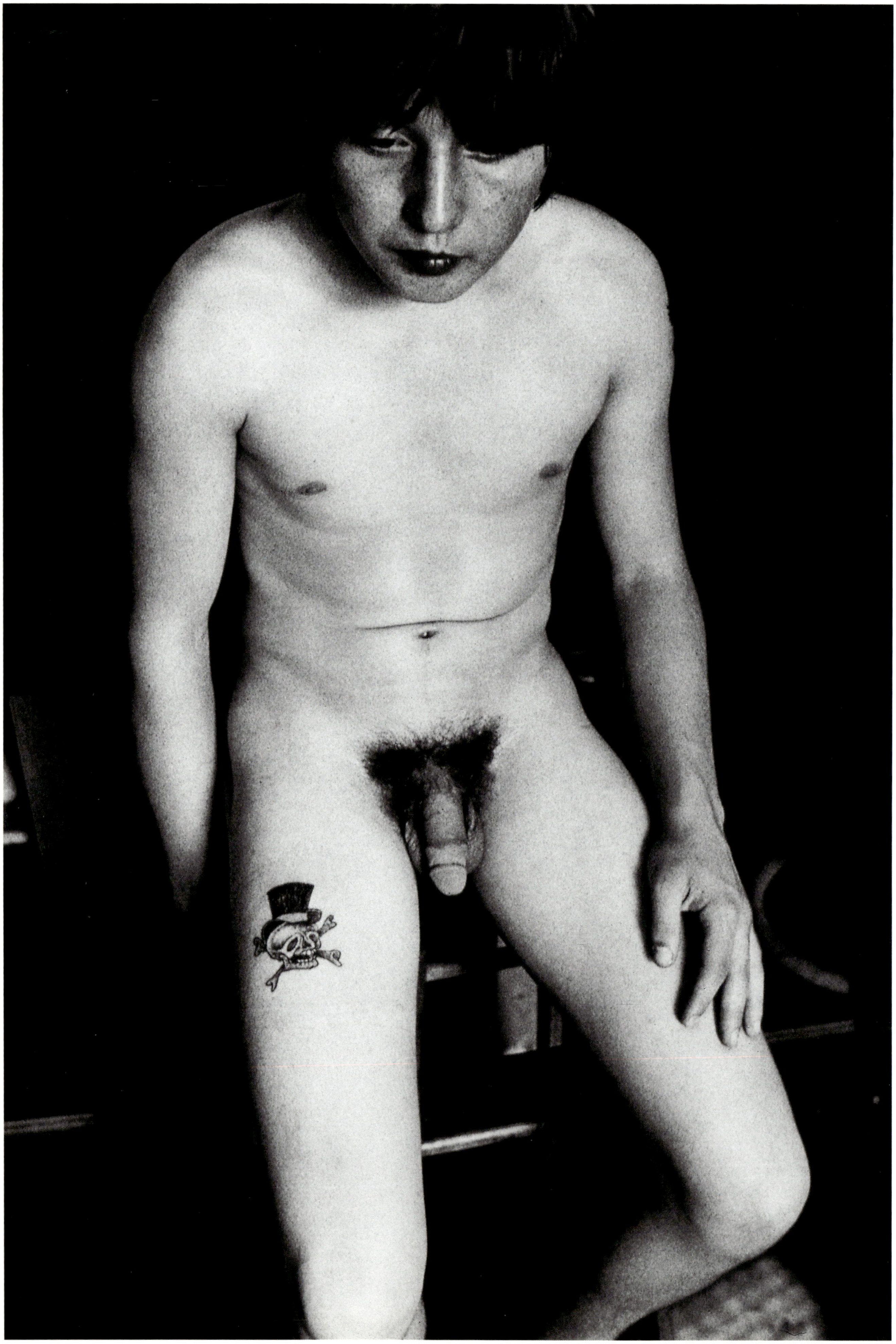

Larry Clark: Outlaw Artist

The criminal like the artist is a social explorer.

—Marshall McLuhan statement from a Larry Clark collage

The outlaw, whether Western gunslinger or Prohibition-era gangster, is one of the defining myths of American culture. We display a certain tolerance towards outlaws as mythic figures; larger than life, they act out forbidden desires we cannot fulfil in our daily lives. At times they are even cheered on as popular opposition to societal norms. The myths, however, are usually not reports from the margins but created in the heart of society. The myth of the outlaw was born historically more as a projection from the East than a record of the West, perhaps as a fantasy response to personal failure of the American Dream.

Usually the criminal shares the conditions of everyone else, in spite of Larry Clark's "code of the outlaw": "I've always made a point not to work. I will not work."[1] The criminal is internal to society and defined by his relationship to society. That symbiotic relationship to authority, of cop to criminal, has been the stuff of pulp fiction and Hollywood film. The outlaw, however, derives his mythic power from that position on the border between inside and outside.

How appropriate to have an artist in this exhibition who has led an outlaw existence—not that he came to art as rehabilitation in prison; Clark produced his art while he was on the loose as an outlaw. And what he has photographed has become a defining vision. His first book of photographs, *Tulsa*, gathered in three forays to his home town in 1963, 1968, and 1971, and published that last year, is now a classic on the order of *The Americans* by Robert Frank. But Clark's vision is also seen as contaminating, and it has elicited a panicky response, most recently with the 1995 release of his feature-length film, *Kids*: "Is the new Miramax bombshell, *Kids*, an honest glimpse into the lives of lost children? Or the perverse vision of the 21-year-old who wrote it and the legendary outlaw artist who directed it?" was a typical headline, here of an article in *New York* magazine.[2]

Tulsa developed from Clark's experiences with family and friends in that city. His mother was a door-to-door baby photographer whom Clark assisted, first as a salesman and then as a photographer himself, beginning when he was sixteen. Used to having his camera with him, and accustomed to making people look good in order to make a sale, Clark discovered that his companions were willing subjects and eager to see the images as he produced them. "I've never been a distanced observer, it's always been autobiographical. I was just one of the people, one of the guys. I happened to have a camera because my parents had this baby-photography business. When I was out with friends, shooting drugs, I would have my equipment with me, because I would be coming from or going to work. I think *Tulsa* worked so well because it was a natural thing. I was part of the scene, with no motive to cap on my friends or anything."[3]

When he started shooting amphetamine at sixteen, he was part of the 1950s drug scene. While we now know this milieu from the Beat literature of the likes of Kerouac and Burroughs or from that of Hubert Selby Jr., theirs was clandestine, not the popular drug culture it would become in the 1960s. Speed was the drug of choice for Clark's friends. The drug that was to stimulate activity at Warhol's Factory and elsewhere during the 1960s was available in the form of the amphetamine in Valo, a nasal inhaler purchased for a dollar in drugstores. The large amount of amphetamine in it could be worked up and injected.

"I was born in Tulsa, Oklahoma in 1943. When I was sixteen I started shooting amphetamine. I shot with my friends every day for three years and then left town but I've gone back through the years. Once the needle goes in it never comes out."[4] This was a life already established before Clark went to art school, and it would be the impetus for the images recorded later in *Tulsa*. The "heroes" of Clark's book are his drug buddies, as well as those named in the book,

Billy Mann and David Roper, bad boys who would either OD or end in pentitentiary. With Clark, as high school students, they were the first wave of youth disobedience, otherwise known as juvenile delinquency, that became epidemic during the 1950s, spawning books and movies (*The Wild One* [1954], *Rebel without a Cause* [1955], *Blackboard Jungle* [1955], *I Was a Teenage Werewolf* [1957] and other JD exploitation films concentrating on bad boys and bad girls. Warhol's *Vinyl* was a 1960s version with its own perverse twist). Following on congressional hearings on organized crime and Communist infiltration, juvenile delinquency had its own Senate Subcommittee hearing to address this more widespread threat of "the enemy within." Beats, bikers, and JDs were the first signs of the breakdown of the American postwar consensus. Significantly, at least for the story Larry Clark likes to tell about his youth, societal blame was laid on parental neglect.

Sent to school in Milwaukee for professional training in commercial photography, Clark, the hipster hoodlum among the crewcuts and bow-ties in the photography department, discovered the other part of the art school and its Beatnik students. He was introduced both to photography as art as well as to *Life* magazine–style 1950s documentary photography, the type advocated by Eugene Smith. Reacting against both the commercialism of one pole of photographic practice and the abstract pictorialism of the other, Clark realized he had another subject to photograph and a story to tell. "One day I snapped, hey, you know, I know a story that no one's ever told, never seen, and I've lived it. It's my own story and my friends' story. I would go back to Oklahoma and start photographing my friends."[5] It was a story of "drugs and violence and rhythm and blues" and it would be called *Tulsa*.

Back in Tulsa through 1963–64, Clark started the first images that made the book. Then, after leaving Tulsa for New York, he was drafted and served for two years in the army, only to be discharged in the midst of the countercultural, rock-and-roll, hippie drug scene of the Lower East Side in New York. At that point he was shooting smack. He showed up in Tulsa in 1968 to make more images, mainly 16 mm film strips that appear in the middle of the book. Clark actually intended *Tulsa* to be a movie and returned at Christmas 1970 for one last attempt at filming. (One episode of filming ended in his arrest on a marijuana-possession charge.) Living with prostitutes and scoring drugs through them, he eventually had to leave town because of the heat, which caused the whole scene to disperse. Then, once again, after kicking around the country, and hearing that Tulsa was shaking, his old friends Roper and Mann back in action and a new drug scene happening, he returned to finish and publish *Tulsa* in 1971, the "hot" period that provided about half the images in the book after he had given up his idea of a movie.

Tulsa has been met with the same moralism that greeted *The Americans* (and at about the same time as the publication of *Tulsa*, the photographs of Diane Arbus). A generally complimentary review on its publication ("A Devastating Portrait of an American Tragedy"[6]) noted the grim, lacerating look at the failure of the American Dream with its victims—at their own hands or those of others—vacant and self-destructive. But would a participant who recorded this scene "with a ferocious honesty" believe that self-destruction was what he was representing? In these photographs, Clark tried to recreate the seductive appeal of film noir and the drama of B-movies. These were his friends, and he wanted to make them appear attractive. That love shows, in the 1963 section of the book, in his tender portraits of his male friends in self-absorbed reveries in front of mirrors or alone in cars. The drug scenes repeat that personal absorption in the moments before or after shooting up, and the group scenes exude the sheer rapture of fixing and shooting and experiencing the rush of the drug. Clark does not approach the drug scene as a moralist but as a participant who tries to capture the exhilaration of what Lou Reed expressed in his period song "Heroin" (1967) when he sang "when I'm rushing on my run/and I feel just like Jesus' son." But Clark didn't flinch from recording the violence and death itself. Guns and violence begin to obtrude in the 1971 section of the book.

After *Tulsa* was published, Clark returned to Oklahoma. His outlaw days began in earnest. Once again, he lived off prostitutes, scored his drugs from their tricks, got involved in petty crime, knifings, shootings, and was arrested for shoplifting, charged with assault and battery, drunk driving, possession of guns, and so on—"Oklahoma shit, man. Just normal Oklahoma shit." The drugs, the petty crime, the desultory life and its violence, the "normal Oklahoma shit," have been well portrayed in Denis Johnson's *Jesus' Son*, stories set approximately in this period. Clark was sentenced to five years in penitentiary in the mid-1970s and was released after nineteen months.

But in 1973 he was involved with Jack Johnson, one of the "police characters" who appear in his next book *Teenage Lust*. Clark thought he could turn his criminal activity into a new photographic project based on a whorehouse, with "girls and prostitutes and crime and whatever comes up. . . . I'm really trying to take *Tulsa* into another thing. I'm really trying to get into photographing the adult criminal thing. I was going to photograph this . . . a different way of life, shall we say? The adult criminal. And it was not working well. And then Jack dies on me. Son of a bitch. My main subject dies on me."

What he produced instead was *Teenage Lust* (first edition 1983; expanded edition 1987), which consists of outtakes from *Tulsa* and new material ordered autobiographically and nearly chronologically (it is subtitled *An Autobiography by Larry Clark*). Clark has called *Teenage Lust* a scrapbook and *Tulsa* a movie. *Tulsa* reveals a fluid handling of images, as if Clark was directing a sequence of scenes, whereas *Teenage Lust* is more halting, as if he was trying to make sense of his life and to find where these images fitted. (The book concludes with an excoriating confessional, a long first-person text written or recorded as if it was an autobiographical letter from Neal Cassady to Jack Kerouac.) As with *Tulsa*, Clark knew he needed certain material to complete the book, and *Tulsa* had given him the way. Near the end of the first book begins the documentation of the next generation, the younger kids, brothers and sisters of his friends, and their experiences with sex and drugs. So in the early 1970s he started photographing the kids that would henceforth be his enduring theme and trademark. "I knew I had to have a little sex and drugs but I had no idea it was going to turn out to be the kids from next door." The book ends with his release from prison, finally able to leave Tulsa and return to New York, and his discovery in 1979–80 of a new subject—the teenage male hustlers on Forty-second Street. Yet for all his fascination with the young boys, he realized he had come only full circle, which is why he concludes the book with a photograph of a gang bang recalling his activities in Tulsa that he was escaping from.[7]

The artistic dead end of these images perhaps explains why Clark went to such painful lengths to implicate and reveal himself in the long autobiographical statement that accompanies them. Self-exposure is the nature of autobiography, and Clark inserts the narrative of "teenage lust" and his imbricated role in *its* exposure after the fact of his own teenage years, within that of his own story. Later collages from 1989 on became vehicles to further disclose himself (his drug record is available for all to read in one of his untitled collages and a letter to his father in another). They allowed him to work out his obsessions, which would finally freely let loose with *Kids*.

Clark's life and his first two books are legendary and have influenced Hollywood's own depictions and mythologizing of the criminal margins and its use of younger and younger actors. One of its directors, Gus Van Sant, was influenced by Clark, and Van Sant's *Drugstore Cowboy* gives

Clark's books a credit at the end of the movie. Never satisfied with Hollywood's representation of teenagers, Clark made his own movie, *Kids*. The outraged journalistic reaction to *Kids* points to the moral panic in society and its concern that its youngsters are criminally out of control. It is not so much Clark's life, which was re-mythologized with the advance notice for this film, as his *depictions* that threaten, as if people fear a contagion from the images of what already exists. (Not that these are made up or reflect only Clark's perverse desires. He has spoken consistently of wanting to go back and re-do his teenage years; his desire has always been more to *be* than to *possess* the teenage subjects of his images.) The parental panic that is not represented within *Kids*—it's their own story—is prefigured in Clark's collages, which incorporate newspaper stories and photographs. By means of these readily available materials, Clark works out his own obsessions while at the same time registering widespread anxiety about teenage sexuality and the moral inversions that could lead to violence and murder, even of parents.

In most cases, the collages also include copy and images from teen fan magazines and other print ephemera, juxtaposed with some of Clark's own photographs. These arrangements are not collages, strictly speaking, since the diverse materials are pinned side by side on the walls, not combined and confined in a circumscribed format. As a result, some of the more crowded walls of images look like those in teenagers' rooms. Much as the pictures of James Dean and Marlon Brando and the biker regalia on the bedroom wall of Kenneth Anger's biker protagonist in his *Scorpio Rising* allowed the filmmaker to create a psychological profile for his gang leader, so Clark assembles his talismans of teenage desire. An untitled collage from 1990 shows images of sex and death together with photographs and clippings of various "bad boy" rock stars from Elvis, the Rolling Stones, Johnny Thunders and Stiv Bators to boxers, the actor Robert De Niro from *Taxi Driver*, the comedian Lenny Bruce, Christ, and the porn star Annie Sprinkle, among others. But it is the two newspaper clippings, with their headlines "Spat drove teen to kill Mom: DA" and "Teen 'just wanted love'" that delineate Clark's preoccupations: the killer kid next door, the child who acts out a revenge on the parents.

What society fears, and fears to expose, motivates Clark as the very truths it can no longer suppress:

> I was thinking about things you couldn't photograph. How are you going to document a kid killing his parents? How are you going to be there when a kid dies from autoerotic asphyxiation? The collages were a way for me to deal with that problem, to tell the story in another way. I started mixing up all this teenage stuff—the perfect childhood done by Hollywood, by the media, by all the stuff we read and see, with the way childhood was supposed to be in the fifties when I was a kid, the way it wasn't at all.
>
> I'd been seeing all these newspaper stories about kids murdering their parents but the kids didn't look right. They always looked twisted or older than seventeen, but this kid looked perfect. He's got his Motley Crue t-shirt, the jean jacket, the long hair, and just a wisp of moustache. This is how I want a killer kid to look, like the kid next door.[8]

Noland's free-standing swings (wickedly titled *PUBLYCK SCULPTURE*, suggesting that the first public sculptures were public stocks) now find resonance in their duplication in the silkscreened images of the backyard garbage dumps of the white-trash Manson family (see *TRASHING FOLGERS*). As society's markers, eastern stocks and western gallows represent two orders of society: the internal repression and closed order of the East, and the open society and rough justice of the expanding frontier. The lawful and the lawless are articulated around these symbols of order and disorder. (The end of the 1960s, meanwhile, is presided over by the dual symbols of law and disorder of Charles Manson and Richard Nixon.)

This consummate outsider—petty criminal, car thief, pimp—the psychopath and con man Charles Manson was ripe for transformation from outlaw to celebrity when he became a murderer or orchestrator of murder. Immediately, he became a symbol, as Joan Didion wrote in *The White Album*: "Many people I know in Los Angeles believe that the Sixties ended abruptly on August 9, 1969, ended at the exact moment when word of the murders on Cielo Drive traveled like bushfire through the community, and in a sense this was true."[2] A symbol that can galvanize is also a symbol that is ambivalent and open for transformation, and Manson's mythologization continues today in the revivals of interest in his crimes, his personality, and his music.

In choosing Manson, Noland has isolated an icon who is also a transformative figure. (The ultimate outsider is the trickster.) He became celebrated by a violent act on another celebrity, thereby transforming himself from a nobody into a somebody. But I think she has also selected Manson because he is an outlaw who is both psychopath and con man. The con man and psychopath are outsiders who play the game of the insider and seek to control that game to the detriment (and sometimes death) of the other.[3] If the con man declines to operate within society, he still duplicates the corporate model; if he no longer plays the game, he still reproduces its conformity. He becomes the outsider who gathers a sect around him, usually disguised as a religious community—with David Koresh and Waco being the contemporary example of the communitarian ideal in American history. Society fears the sacrifice of its sons and daughters to the charismatic figure. Towards the icon, which brings disorder into some semblance of order, gravitate its disenfranchised youth. Around the Manson icon circulate the Manson girls—the girls from next door.

That we tend to focus on Manson more than on the "family" shows the media transformation that is so essential to demonizing the outsider. These operations are representative of a deep need in the American psyche and are a dominant aspect of American culture since Puritan days. The nature of celebrity is intertwined with the theme of outsider, and both partake of the same mythologizing process.

Much of Noland's work deals with the binary opposition of outlaw and celebrity and the transformative act that changes one into the other. Such pairs in her work as, for example, Oswald/Kennedy and Manson/Tate, now stand as signs of the historic episodes of the 1960s (with the dates 1963 and 1969 opening and closing the decade as an idea). Although she favours only one part of the dyad—the outlaw who becomes a celebrity himself—the two are forever indissolubly wed (just as Oswald and Ruby are forever bound in the instant and image of the familiar Robert Jackson photograph of Jack Ruby shooting Oswald). As celebrity outlaw, Patty Hearst unites the two categories, but there must be some characteristic in each that originally binds the two—celebrity and outlaw—to each other.

In a 1990 interview, Cady Noland suggested that violence once had a positive role and reputation in American life. What was once an element of political agency now is only an individual outlet that reflects a lack of political organization and represents instead the venting of hostility and envy "without threatening the structures of society." Still other aspects of "violence" to the individual have a social role when she suggests that tabloid "trashing helps to dampen people's anger over their situation or their own place in the hierarchy of importance."[4]

Even as an outsider, the outlaw plays a key societal role, not only as a transformative agent through his acts of violence but as a structural figure that articulates the boundaries of inside and outside. Although violence stems from the individual, we could say violence is a social function. If the celebrity—or rather the icon of the celebrity, since we are really dealing with images—attracts violence (as the history of assassination from John Kennedy to John Lennon makes clear), violence is thus intimately linked to representation. It could be argued that violence makes the icon as it unmakes the individual. Violence and the icon are as intimately linked as the celebrity and outlaw.

In this regard, Cady Noland was on to something, whether she knew it or not, when in 1993 she said, "I'm interested in the differences and similarities between blank identity and iconography as well as anonymity and fame." She spoke of these oppositions in relation to the American landscape and America's tolerance for the temporary, for the ad hoc vernacular of its roadsides, for the American highways with their garages, junkyards, and cars on cinder blocks, things in states of construction or decay next to the "beautiful Gestalt" of the American flag or the "palliative Gestalt images" of advertising logos such as Coca-Cola. "I try sometimes to construct a mirror of that weird stuff that doesn't fit together, floating in a sea of palliative Gestalt images. People are able to live with the scattered and fragmented stuff because they are always reassured by the concept or the image of things that are whole."[5]

Fragmentation and wholeness exist within the same reality, and a need is expressed for both. Their cohabitation suggests both a tolerance and a necessity. Wholeness assures fragmentation and fragmentation wholeness. However, what is born in and of that fragmentation, chaos, and lack confronts wholeness with a vengeance bordering on destruction. Destruction, not the reassurance of the Gestalt, is the palliative here.

If we can extend the intuition that blank identity is to iconography as anonymity is to fame, then we can interrogate not only the relation of each term to its other but the relation of one set to the other, as well. In turn, they become the grid for interpreting Noland's works. In this light, compare *TRASHING FOLGERS* with its image of the chaotic garbage heap of the Manson backyard or *BIBLE AMONG THE GARBAGE* to the Gestalt media icons of Manson, such as *MR. SIR*. Even in his collapsing state, *OOZEWALD* (Oswald) among the heap of materials in Noland's 1989 installation *Deep Social Space* (p. 26) asserts the same relationship of icon to surrounding, Gestalt to fragment.

Fragmentation is to Gestalt as violence is to honorific expenditure or waste—the wasting or degrading of the icon. As the outlaw becomes celebrity, the celebrity is trashed; one is elevated and the other degraded. The outlaw marks the divide between, on the one side, the indifferentiated outside, the site of lack of identity and chaos (blank identity and anonymity) and, on the other side, iconography and fame. The outlaw is to celebrity as violence is to the icon. The outlaw articulates the moment between violence and representation and is caught himself in its iconic constructions.

Notes

1 "There is a method in my work which has taken a pathological trend. From the point at which I was making work out of objects I became interested in how, actually, under which circumstances people treat other people like objects. I became interested in psychopaths in particular, because they objectify people in order to manipulate them. By extension they represent the extreme embodiment of a culture's proclivities; so psychopathic behavior provides useful highlighted models to use in search of cultural norms." "Cady Noland," *Journal of Contemporary Art* 3: 2 (1990): 22–23.

2 Joan Didion, *The White Album* (New York: Simon and Schuster, 1979), 46.

3 "A critique of the psychopathic ideal. Yes, it's the model of the entrepreneurial male whose goals excuse any and all sorts of egregious behaviour if those goals meet with success." "Metal Is a Major Thing to Waste: Interview with Cady Noland," *Archis* (January 1994): 78. See as well Noland, "Towards a Metalanguage of Evil," *documenta* IX (Stuttgart: Edition Cantz, 1992), III, 410–413.

4 "Cady Noland," *Journal of Contemporary Art*: 21, 22. "Figures like the one with the bullet holes refer to clippings—to the way celebrities are being treated in 'scandal-sheets' like *The Globe*. They are manipulated in a very violent but childlike way. Blowing that up is a way of making the violence more manifest." "Metal Is a Major Thing to Waste," 80.

5 "Metal Is a Major Thing to Waste," 79.

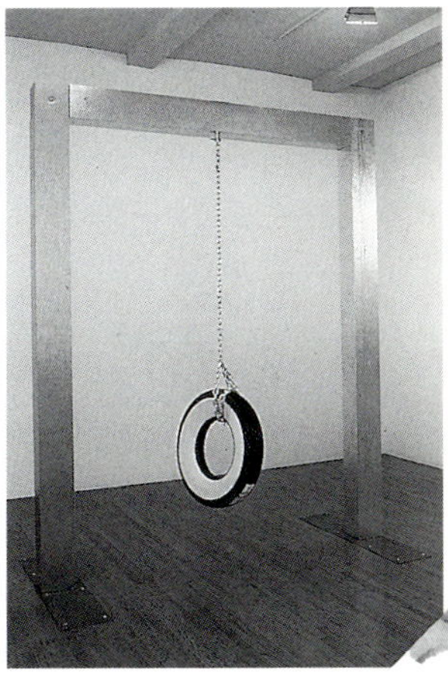

ABOVE
Cady Noland
MY AMUSEMENT. 1993–94

BELOW
BELTWAY TERROR. 1993–94

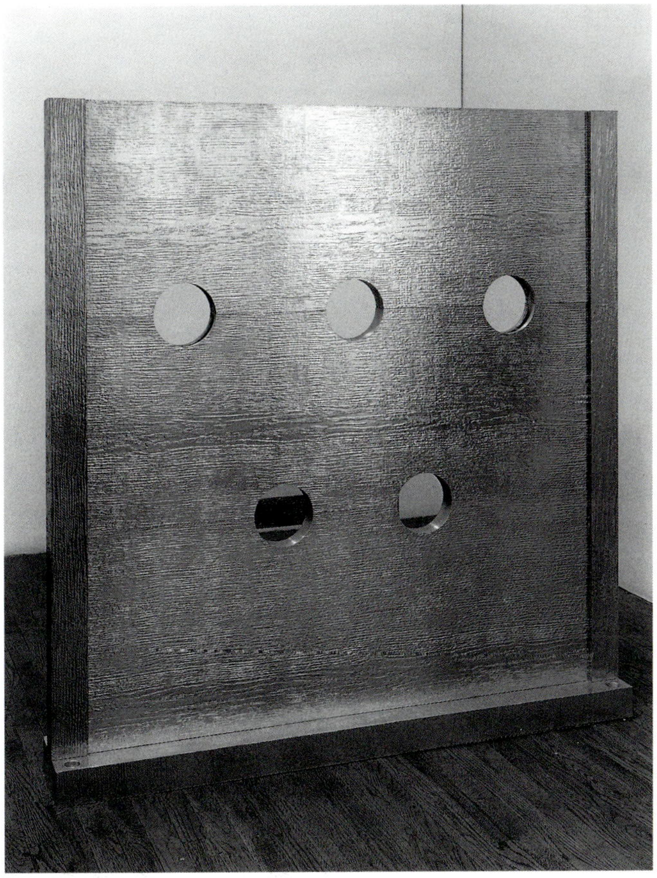

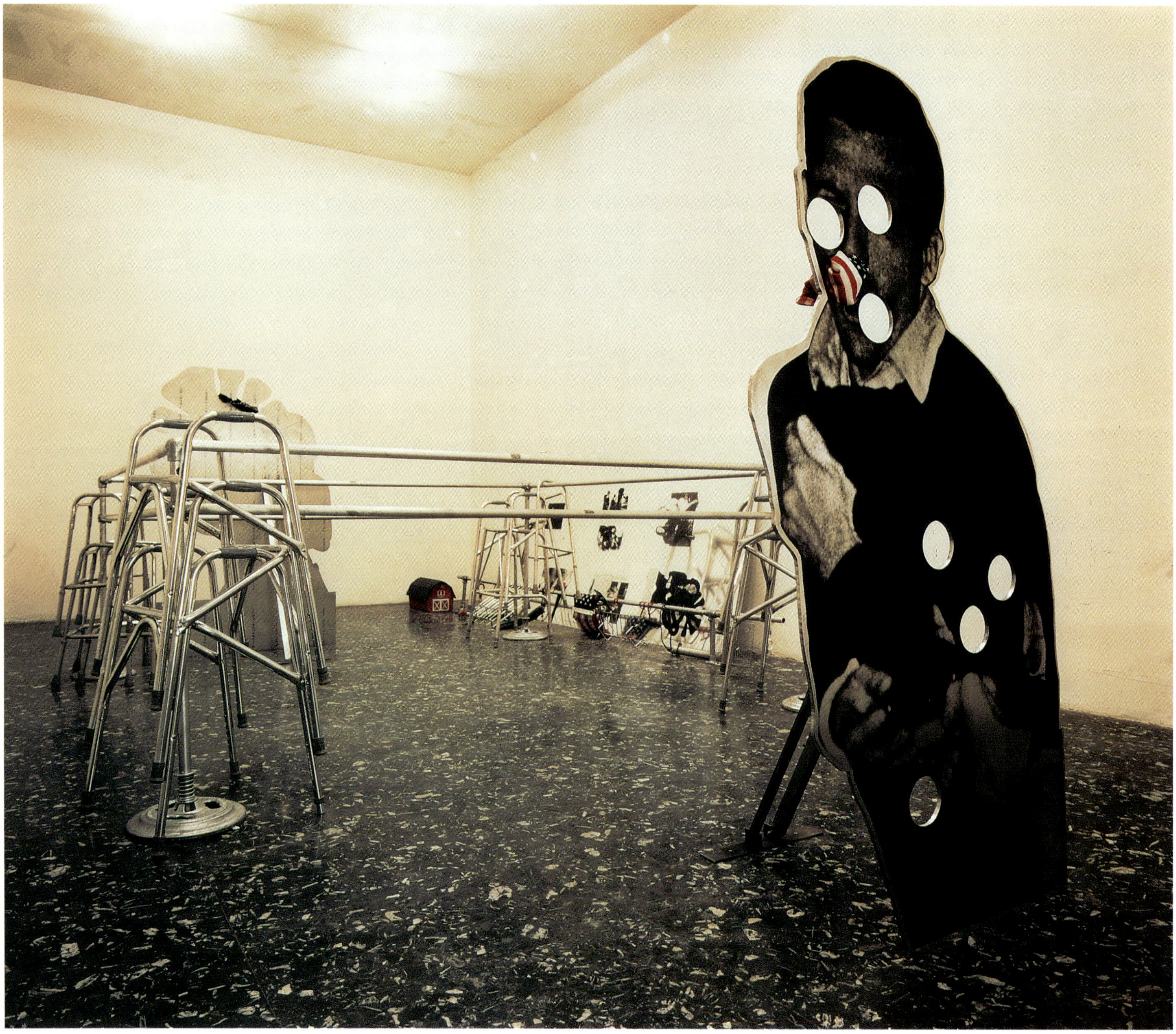

Cady Noland

Deep Social Space installation (detail: *OOZEWALD. FRAME DEVICE*), 1989

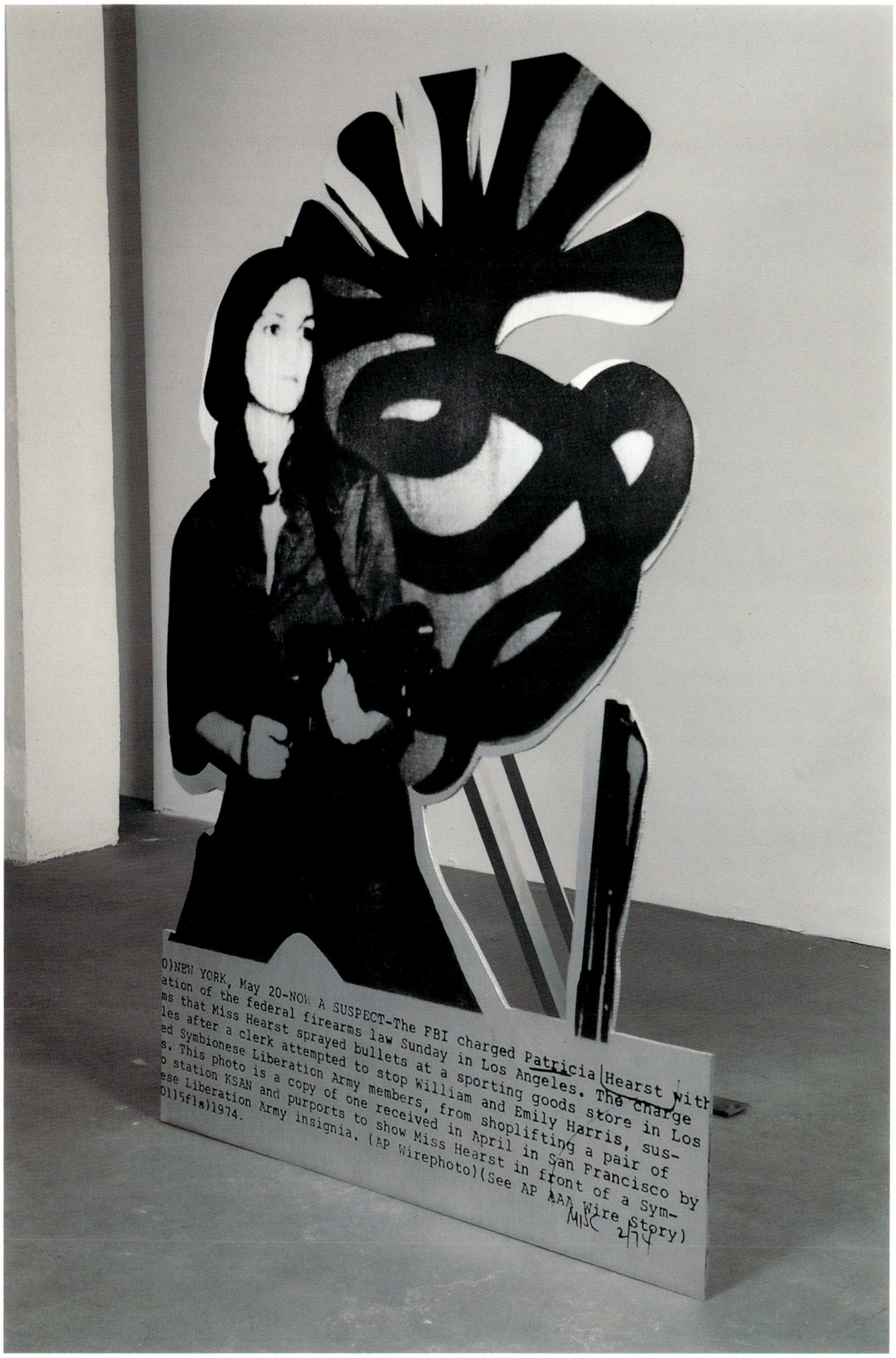

TANYA AS A BANDIT. 1989

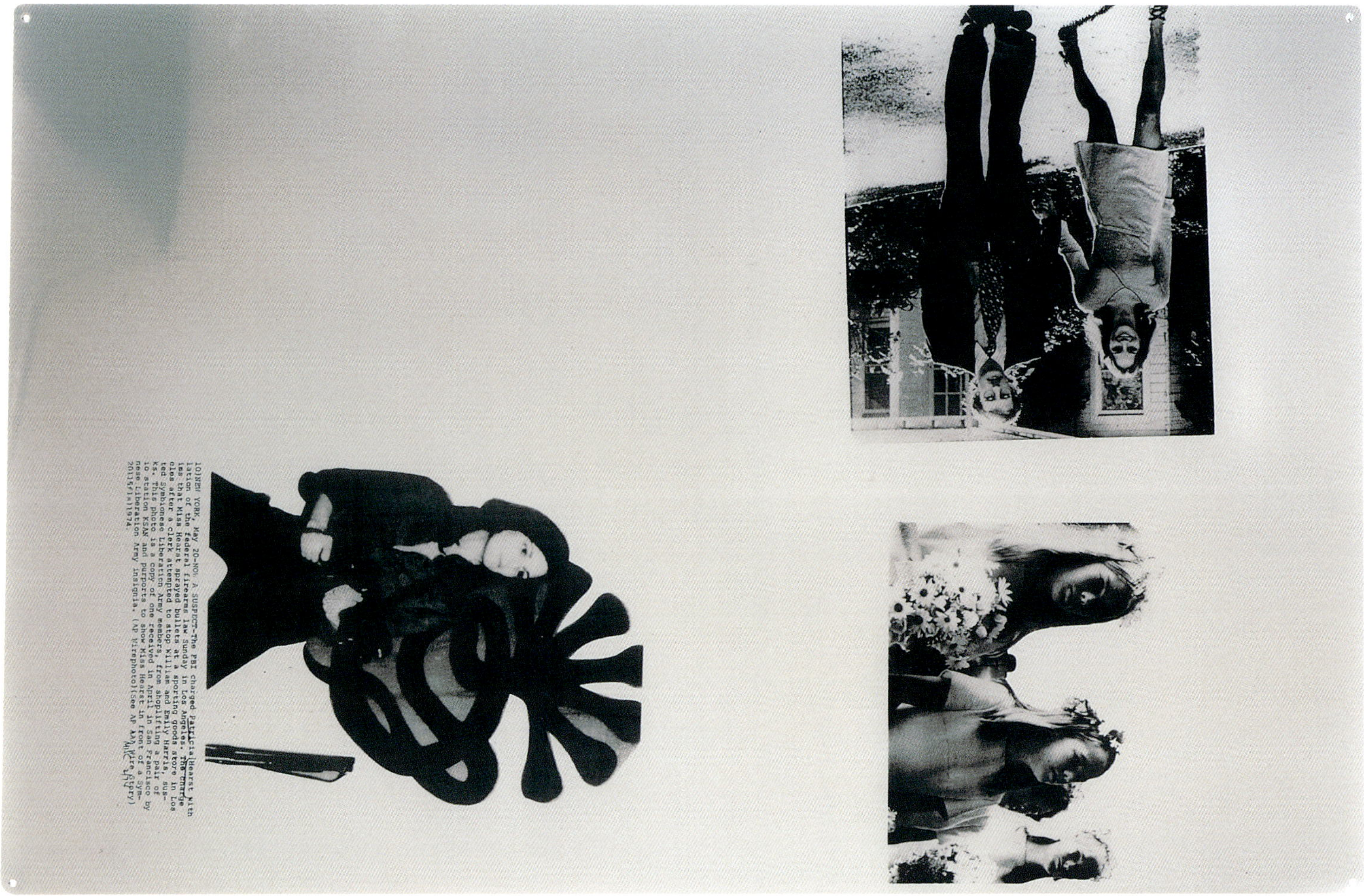

UNTITLED. 1989

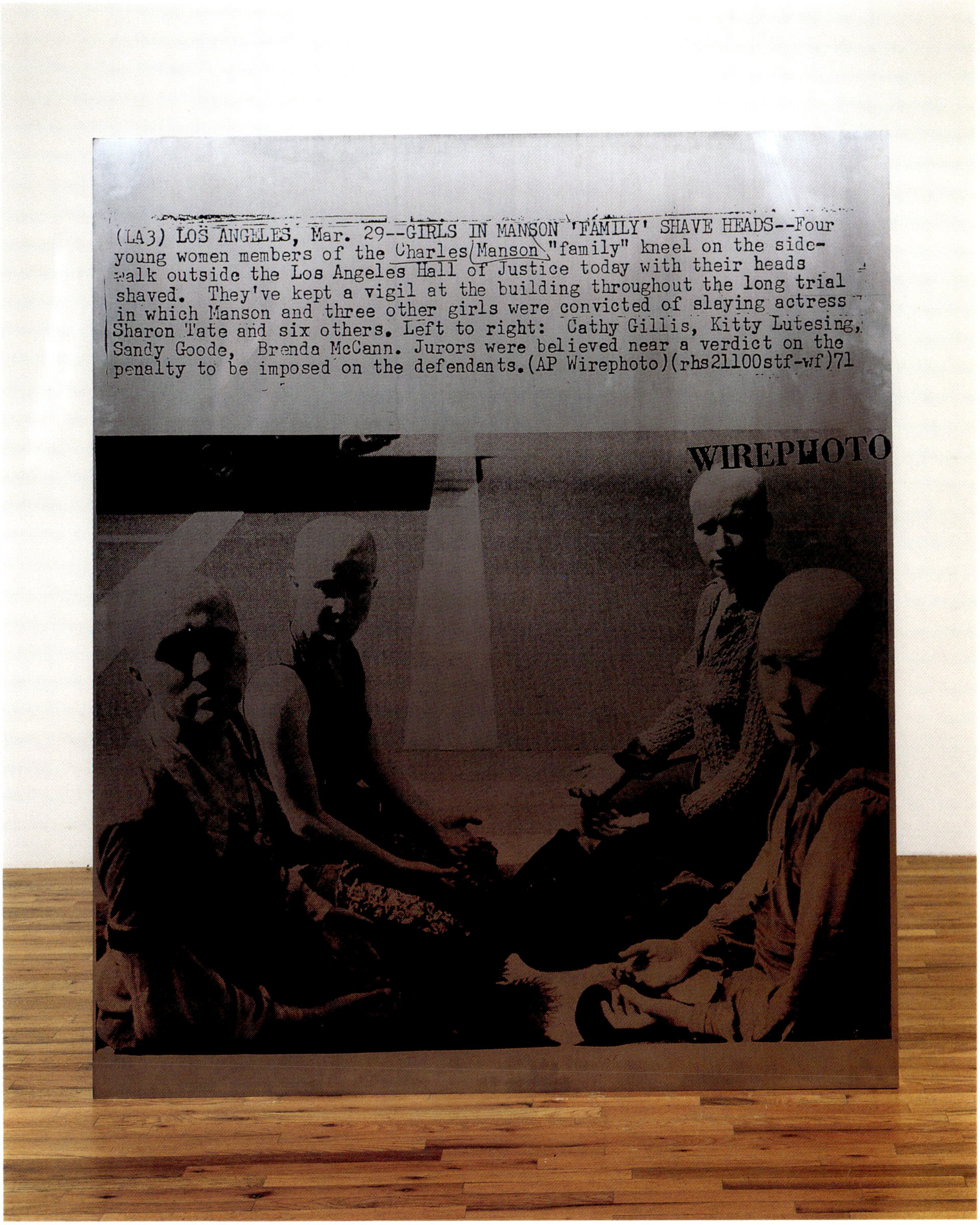

(NOT YET TITLED). 1994

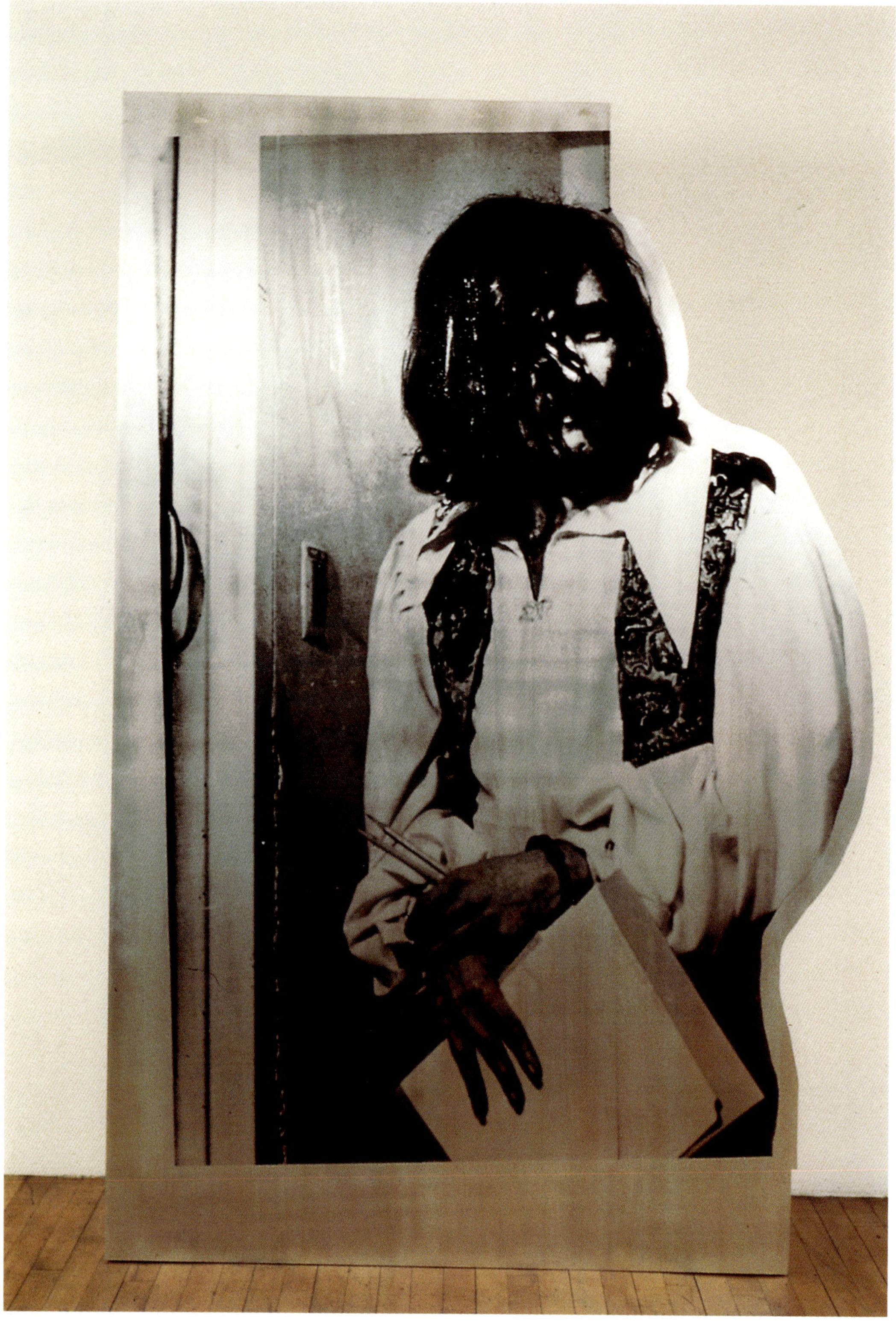

MR. SIR. 1993

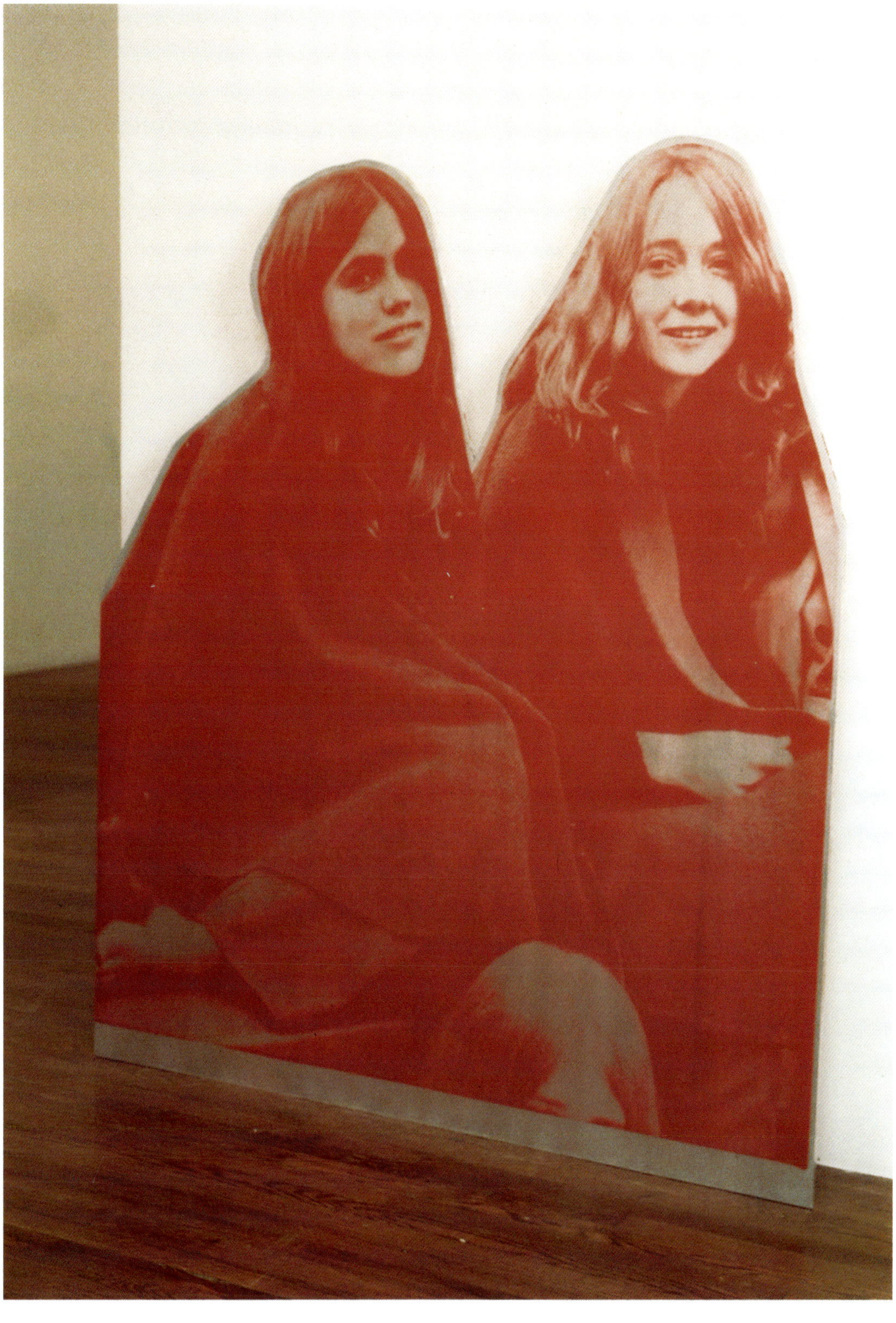

MANSON GIRLS 'SIT-IN'. 1993–94

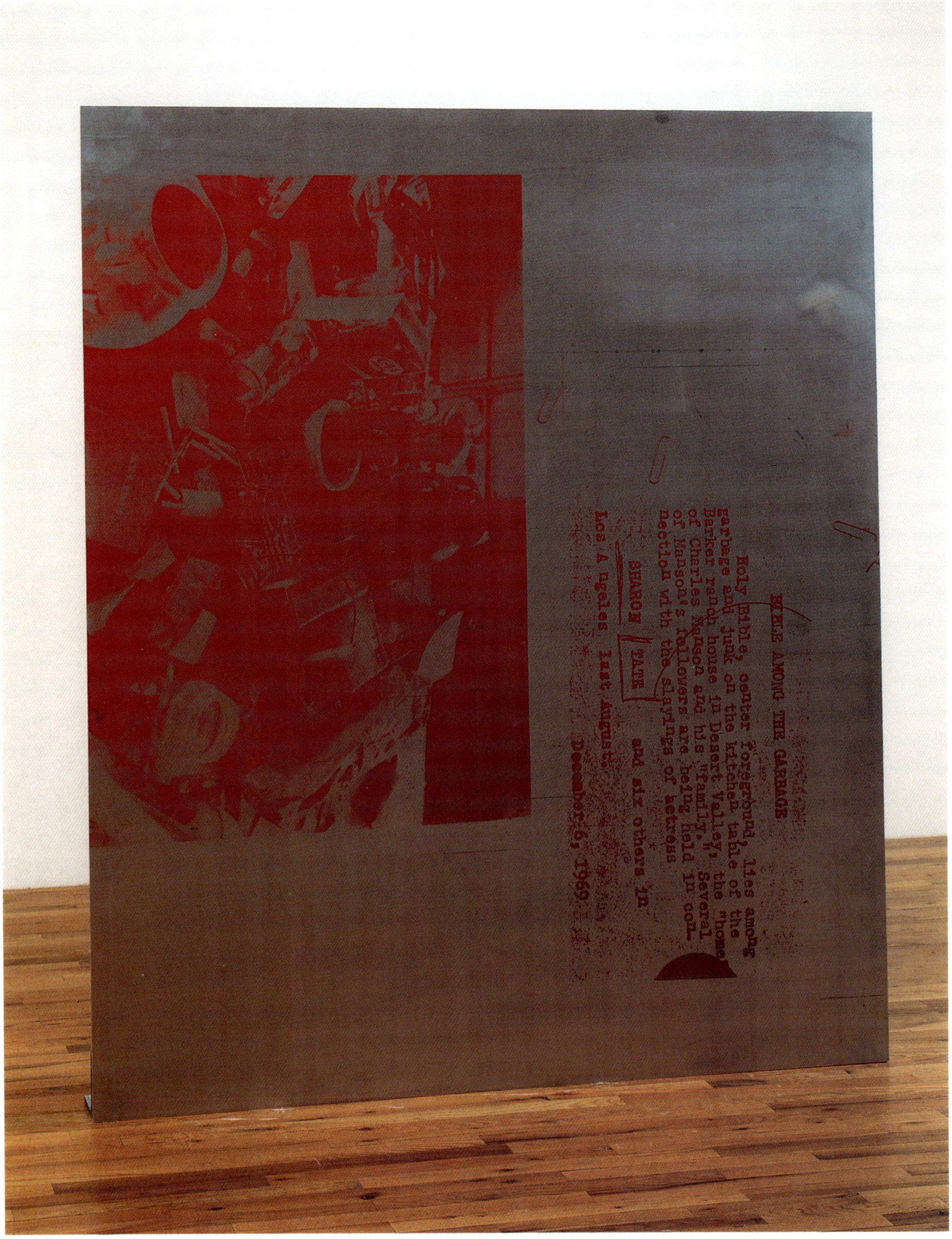

BIBLE AMONG THE GARBAGE. 1993–94

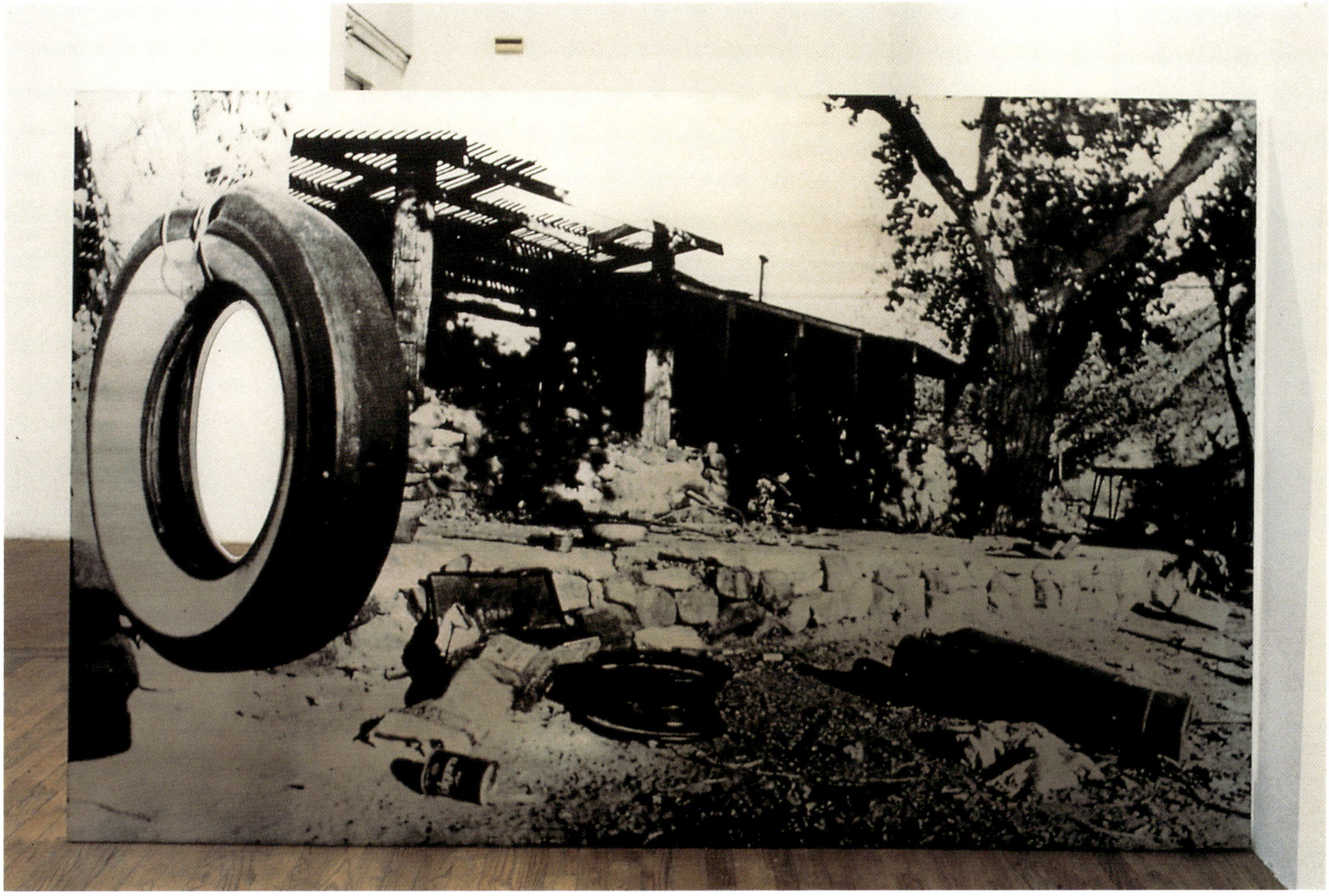

TRASHING FOLGERS. 1993–94

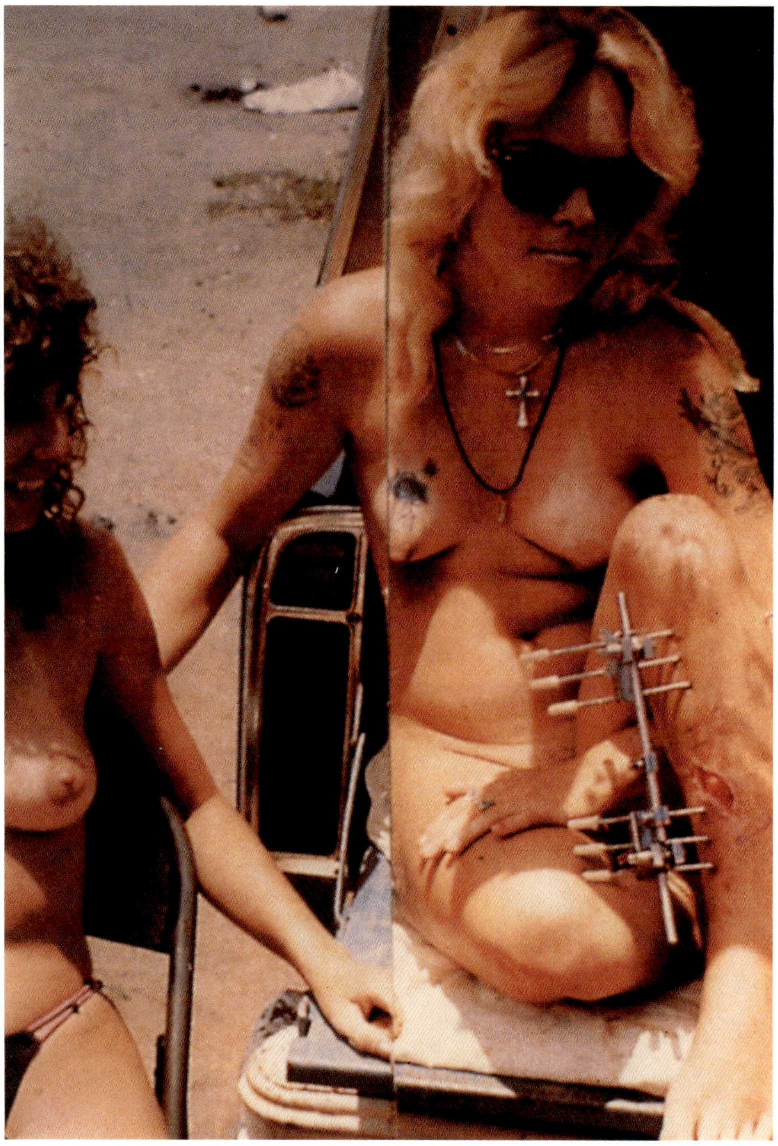

Richard Prince
Untitled (Party) 1994

Richard Prince: Live Free or Die

Summer of Love

I am writing this essay taking a hint from scattered cues in Richard Prince's writings and interviews, as if two turntables were playing on either side of me, mixing and blurring sounds and images from another era. On my left, something from the Beach Boys, circa 1966–67, perhaps *Pet Sounds*; on my right, the Velvet Underground, probably *The Velvet Underground and Nico*, produced by Andy Warhol, from 1967. Asked in the interview "Richard Prince Tells All," a title that should put us on our guard to whatever verity is to be revealed or secret confessed, "What would be the soundtrack to the book *Spiritual America*?", Prince answered, "Something that's a cross between the Velvet Underground and the Beach Boys."[1]

Spiritual America (1989) is that typical publication by Prince, more an artist's book than a catalogue; although it accompanied an exhibition, there is no critical or curatorial text, for instance. It functions like a magazine, mixing Prince's own works with images from surfing, car, skin, biker, and joke magazines, themselves the sources of his pictorial works and subject to modifications of rephotography here. In that sense, the interviewer's question was apt: What aural sampling would match Prince's visual mix?

A taste that encompasses both the Velvet Underground and the Beach Boys can be imagined, since the music of both are first, and above all, commercial products available for purchase, however their images may be marketed to individual tastes, desires, and identifications. Earlier, in one of his stories in his 1983 book, *Why I Go to the Movies Alone*, Prince attributed this bilateral taste to a woman character:

> She had never qualified the two groups and never tried to figure out why she received pretty much of the same kind of satisfaction from what could have been easily described as sounds and images from two different worlds.
>
> Again she just thought the worlds were interesting and there was, she felt, no reason she couldn't be a citizen of both.
>
> This of course is not to say she wasn't aware of the blackness, the leather, the shininess of the Underground . . . or the sunshine, surf, and sand, associated with the Beachboys. But she knew too that these things were descriptions, ways of fabricating a sense (surrounding the attraction), a way to put your finger on them and make whatever they were supposed to be, easier to swallow . . .[2]

The Velvet Underground and the Beach Boys serve as aural exemplars, corresponding to the West and East Coasts of the country, the mainstream and underground scenes of 1960s Los Angeles and New York City. Their sounds signify two different worlds, a difference made apparent when the Velvet Underground played L.A. for the first time in 1966. But just as the two cannot be dissolved into each other like the free-floating graphic effects of a psychedelic poster or melded together as in the sensory effects of the light-show happenings of Warhol's Exploding Plastic Inevitable or Kesey's Pranksters' Acid Tests, neither do they stand merely as opposites, representing the two different trips of "shiny boots of leather" or beach, babes, and boards. Differences of description may make them "easier to swallow" if we think of them as opposites; the dissonance of thinking them together reveals another picture. (Is it a coincidence that behind these two bands hover the master manipulators of the two coasts: Charles Manson and Andy Warhol?)

What these differences or descriptions "mean" is perhaps what they initially *refer* to. (For Prince, meaning is a joke.) For instance, *Spiritual America* "republishes" the purported interview of Prince by J. G. Ballard, titled "Extraordinary." The preposterousness of this interview hasn't failed to sucker one senior critic: its fictional status is readily apparent from its intentional chronological inconsistencies and other embedded clues. The interview is carefully dated 1967, August 1967 to be exact. Carefully, I say, because Prince has also worked that impossible date into later compositions.

We might think that the interview and redating are merely tactics in Prince's elaborate strategies of constructing identity through masks. They are, of course. More important, however, this date (during the Summer of Love) becomes the reference point for the selection ("cropping," we could say) and circulation of particular images, sounds, and texts that fabricate the sense surrounding *his* attraction.

His attraction, however, cannot fail to be marked by historical traces and current obsessions. He has elsewhere called his art "social science fiction," so it might here be reclassified "historical fiction." Because Prince simply selects views and does not judge through his images, because his works encompass such a variety of references and media (the gangs, the joke paintings, the hoods, and so on), and because his work was initially read as a critique of commodity representation and taken to be *the* appropriationist exemplar, this historicizing tendency has not been readily apparent. Even if his work appears merely to repeat or increase that flow of images from our media age, nevertheless, in reproducing images, his work produces a history. More than a semiology of the image carried out through the image alone, collectively his works picture our history.

Maybe he seeks this understanding for himself alone. In this, his would be opposite the more public career of Oliver Stone and his siftings of the sights and sounds of the 1960s—public, because Stone manipulates icons already loaded with meaning, marking each mythic moment with a succession of historical figures from JFK to Richard Nixon—that is, from the origins to the end of American involvement in Vietnam. (The baroque montages, mixing image and sound, history and fiction, of Francis Ford Coppola's *Apocalyse Now* and Kenneth Anger's *Scorpio Rising* stand behind Prince's contemporary in film. Where they mix modes, Prince separates them.) Prince's intentions are more oblique. But Prince chose, after all, to set the interview when he was eighteen—the age when he became an adult (the interview documents a rite of passage of sorts) but also when he was legally subject to the draft and to induction into the war in Vietnam. (According to the interview, his psychopathic "father" had a complicit role in defoliating the jungles of Vietnam. Prince's Vietnam piece, *Untitled (War)*, dates from 1986). Prince gives aesthetic form to what are period artefacts, and since they are not his own images, they cannot help being images of history, albeit a particular kind of history, a history from below, a history from the point of view of the grunt, enacted through the degraded images of the mass media, popular culture, and subcultural representations.

Playing to the Decades

"Consider, for example, the fact that Prince has quite carefully and deliberately restaged one of the more attractive dramas of modern America, one acted out in various ways by everyone from F. Scott Fitzgerald to Axl Rose—the story of the outsider, the melancholy, longing one, the town geek, who moves to the big city after high school, studies how to want, and reemerges some years later as a hero of misunderstood cool."[3] In so doing, Prince has reconstructed for us (I am of his generation), through the decades from the 1950s to the present—through the years of our childhood, our adolescence, our "underground" years, and our adulthood—a history of the hip and the square. Consider, then, that within the welter of images at any one moment in Prince's practice, a certain combination of elements may come to signify a decade: the 1950s, the 1960s, the 1970s, and, of course, the 1980s, when, early in the decade, his work first came to attention. The images, the lists of books, bands, and songs, the jokes and the quotations that appear throughout his publications and written on his works all play to the decades. Clipped images and sound bites are the documents of this archive. (Prince's recent book, *Adult, Comedy, Action, Drama*, suggests another set of classifications—that of the movies.)

The 1980s are almost too easy a representation. Prince's first works of appropriated images seem a pure reflection or distillation of that trumped-up era—a collection of commodities and looks. The 1970s are funkier and more low class in its images collected and "classified" in what Prince calls his "gangs" of rephotographed illustrations from speciality magazines: heavy-metal bands, monster trucks, muscle cars, among others. The 1950s, the era of the suburbs, Madison Avenue, and *Playboy*, of course, are widely represented in Prince's joke and cartoon paintings about wives, sex, drinking, and psychiatry. But the fabled decade of the 1960s—how has Prince chosen to represent it?

The End of the Sixties

No one artist in this exhibition specializes in a type of imagery, even though a collective theme is drawn from their work. Richard Prince's work is limited here to the world of bike gangs. Bikers are outlaws, of course, criminals and rejects from society, and they pride themselves on so being. ("They're the Wild Bill Hickoks, the Billy the Kids—they're the last American heroes we have, man," said the custom-car guru, "Big Daddy" Ed Roth.[4]) But bikers, as well, could be seen as one of the autonomous subcultures, with its own codes, symbols, dress—and means of transportation—originating in postwar California but coming to public consciousness during the 1960s. As the most threatening group, before the hippie and drug culture and then affiliated with it, their representation was a demonization in the media. (Although bikers initially were an immediate postwar phenomenon cultivated by returning GIs, and though Prince's images probably date from a later decade, I am letting bikers stand as a symbol of the 1960s, when they broke into popular consciousness, to be either celebrated or reviled.)

The 1960s was the efflorescent period of recognition of subcultures or "statuspheres" as Tom Wolfe, their great heralder, called them. "After World War II, a number of sets of young men in California began to drop out of the rationalized job system and create their own statuspheres. In every case, they made a point of devising new fashions, *role* clothes, to symbolize their new life styles. These were the beats, the motorcycle gangs, the car kids, and, more recently, the rock 'n' roll kids, the surfers, and, of course, the hippies."[5] If Tom Wolfe was their verbal chronicler, Kenneth Anger was their visual stylist. He used his own film footage ironically counterpointed by contemporary hit singles to document the habits, styles, and desires of these new subcultural sets, such as that of Wolfe's "car kids" in the one fragment of his aborted film *Kustom Kar Kommandos* of 1964–65. More influential, though, was Anger's underground classic of 1963, the biker film *Scorpio Rising*, which continued his Luciferian themes of disobedience—now pop cultural rather than esoteric—in a more recognizable image of delinquency.

Just as much as through media hysteria, this interest in bikers could be seen in various "exploitation" films, where under the guise of dealing with social problems, bikers are now celebrated. Anger's *Scorpio Rising* started the process for the 1960s, but his film was presaged by *The Wild One*, the 1954 Method vehicle for Marlon Brando that was based on an actual biker take-over of a town—the 1947 Hollister riot. Anger incorporated the movie footage, significantly through its television broadcast, in *Scorpio Rising*. Roger Corman's 1966 film *The Wild Angels* kicked off the late 1960s biker exploitation films; Dennis Hopper's *Easy Rider*, 1969, attempted to be its countercultural summation.[6] But the phenomenon was not limited to movies alone. The photojournalist Danny Lyon joined the Chicago Outlaw Motorcycle Club and published *The Bikeriders* in 1968; Robert Frank had a couple of mid-1950s images of black bikers in *The Americans*; and Andy Warhol had been screenprinting images of Brando in denim and leather slouching on his motorcycle from *The Wild One* in his paintings dating from 1963 and 1966. The new journalist Hunter Thompson chronicled both the panic that was set off by events in 1964 that propelled the Hell's Angels into public awareness ("the Angels were about to make a publicity breakthrough, by means of rape, on the scale of the Beatles or Bob Dylan")[7] and the "consciousness" of the bikers themselves in his book *Hell's Angels*, his "insider" account published in 1967. (Although one history of America may be written using the story of the Hell's Angels and biker gangs, another history of culture could be written using the genre of biker movies, from Method [*The Wild One*] to underground [Anger and Warhol] to exploitation [Corman] to countercultural [Hopper].)[8]

Bikers were the West Coast "radical chic," who partied with Ken Kesey and his Merry Pranksters and provided the "security" for San Francisco's psychedelic bands, such as the Grateful Dead and Big Brother and the Holding Company. (The counterculture cartoonist R. Crumb incorporated a Hell's Angels Frisco logo of approval on the album cover of Big Brother's "Cheap Thrills.") Now the Angels exist in the public imagination, along with Manson and the family, as the agents of the end of the 1960s: their documented role in the 1969 Altamont concert murder during a Rolling Stones' performance was the West Coast's answer to Woodstock nation, low culture destroying middle-class counterculture. That year 1969 may be called up in a swirl of paranoid images of Altamont and Cielo Drive that parallels those of the conjurations of Anger's film of the same year—*Invocation of My Demon Brother.*

Spiritual America

Prince continues in the tradition of Anger and Wolfe but now without the ostensible motive of disobedience or the pop thrill of discovery. Perhaps this is only because what Anger and Wolfe enthusiastically embraced as an unconscious assault on the privilege of high culture is now the milieu surrounding us: each subculture currently has various forms of commodity dessimination and means of style communication. Raised on the images from the 1960s, Prince is also heir to its attitudes to history and the image. This was the era when the image became the official representative of culture, when the validation of truth passed in its documentary evidence from word to image. From Vietnam to Watergate was the moment of the delegitimation of official explanation and history: the 1969 moon landing was a studio television production, after all. Now *images* are collectively received and shared. "It's almost as if in this culture information touches a chord in us the same way a hit song makes you impulsively keep a beat with everyone else—because you know you're not the only one who thinks the song is great. The commonality of this information retrieval, the fact that we've shared it and think it's somehow part of us, makes us think about the information as a genuine experience."[9] It is not just that images of history and pop tunes now function similarly. They have joined together: images are now linked to sounds, which is why the decade of the 1960s figures so prominently collectively, and why it is so easy to construct the decade fictionally in films (it's already myth). In making his images real, Prince wanted to give them the overdetermined production values of hits: "I like to think that I make 'hit' pictures. I try to put 'I Heard It Through the Grapevine' in my pictures."[10]

The relation to the image, and not just to its content, defines for Prince what is the outlaw. These images are not Prince's own. They are photographed and sent by bikers to speciality magazines; bikers then buy the magazines and consume the images of their girlfriends. Prince enters into the process through the "criminal" act of stealing the image. But he equally consumes the image by means of what *it* projects, what it "imagines," as Prince would say. No critique is implied in his choice of images; the selection has more to do with Prince's attraction to a particular picture: "Since (say) 1949 there has been a whole generation of artists who have grown up with the idea that they can actually have a relationship with an image as if it had an ego or were alive."[11] To the registry of classy images expensively produced for advertising, we can add those from another milieu—that of white trash communicating to itself. No longer does the image represent only icons or events, but (low) types.

Why the attraction to biker chicks? They are part of what Prince claims has always been his subject: "men and women, men and men, women and women." More particularly, with respect to these images, he has said, "Well, as far as the biker chicks are concerned, I just wouldn't mind being one. I've never said that before, but I think that's what I really feel. There's a certain kind of desire and a certain amount of passion. I like what I think they look like, or perhaps what they are. I think many of these pictures have their own egos and they have an imagination of their own. That's my own particular reaction. I also think the biker chick is perhaps a more realistic representation than the Grace Kelly girl-next-door. I mean, the biker chicks *are* the girls next door."[12]

As an outsider in an outsider's world, Prince naturalizes the image of what he is attracted to in order to normalize its reception.[13] To think of the image as being what one is attracted to, as well as what the *image* imagines, may be the essence of Spiritual America. "Spiritual America"—perhaps this today is the American Dream.

Notes

1 "Richard Prince Tells All," *Frieze* 1 (1991): 29.

2 Richard Prince, *Why I Go to the Movies Alone* (New York: Tanam Press, 1983), 45–46.

3 Jim Lewis, "Outside World," *Richard Prince* (New York: Whitney Museum of American Art, 1992), 75.

4 Hunter Thompson, *Hell's Angels* (New York: Ballatine Books, 1967), 72.

5 Tom Wolfe, "The Hair Boys," *The Pump House Gang* (New York: Bantam Books, 1969), 102.

6 "Yet for several years bike movies have constituted a kind of underground folk literature for adolescents, have located an audience and fabricated a myth to exactly express that audience's every inchoate resentment, every yearning for the extreme exhilaration of death. . . . To imagine the audience for whom these sentiments are tailored, maybe you need to have sat in a lot of drive-ins yourself, to have gone to school with boys who majored in shop and worked in gas stations and later held them up. Bike movies are made for these children of vague 'hill' stock who grow up absurd in the West and Southwest, children whose whole lives are an obscure grudge against a world they think they never made. These children are, increasingly, everywhere, and their style is that of an entire generation." Joan Didion, "Notes Toward a Dreampolitik," 1968–70, *The White Album* (New York: Simon and Schuster, 1979), 100–101.

7 Thompson, 25.

8 The latter would be based on acting styles, the school of Corman undercutting the Method system, ironically mediated by the camp portrayals of Jack Smith's and Warhol's films.

9 Richard Prince in Jeffrey Rian, "Social Science Fiction," *Art in America* 75: 3 (March 1987): 94.

10 Richard Prince in David Robbins, *The Camera Believes Everything* (Stuttgart: Edition Patricia Schwarz, 1988), 46.

11 Richard Prince in Stuart Morgan, "Tell Me Everything," *Artscribe International* 73 (January–February 1989): 51.

12 Brian Wallis, "A Conversation with Richard Prince," *Art in America* 81: 11 (November 1993): 117. Of an early image of biker chicks in his 1986 gang *Live Free or Die*, Prince has said: "*Live Free or Die* could be labelled repressive but these women are living on their own terms." Morgan, 50. This interview also has his comments on the girl-next-door image of Brooke Shields, who is incorporated in the gang *Spiritual America, No. 2*, 1988, as well as being the focus of an entire 1983 work entitled *Spiritual America*.

13 "I'm interested when something offensive becomes respected. I'm interested in being taken for granted. You know, marrying the sheriff's daughter." Robbins, 41.

PAGES 40–47

Richard Prince

Live Free or Die 1986
Three Girlfriends, One with Motorcycle 1987–88
Untitled (Girlfriend) 1993
Untitled (Girlfriend) 1993
Untitled (Girlfriend) 1993
Untitled (Girlfriend) 1993
Untitled (Party) 1994
Untitled (Party) 1994

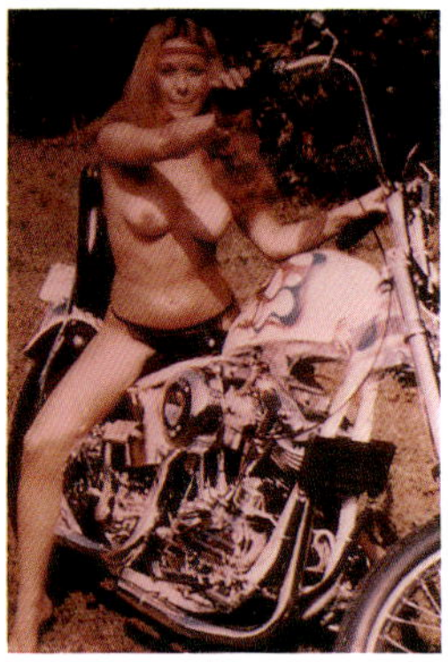

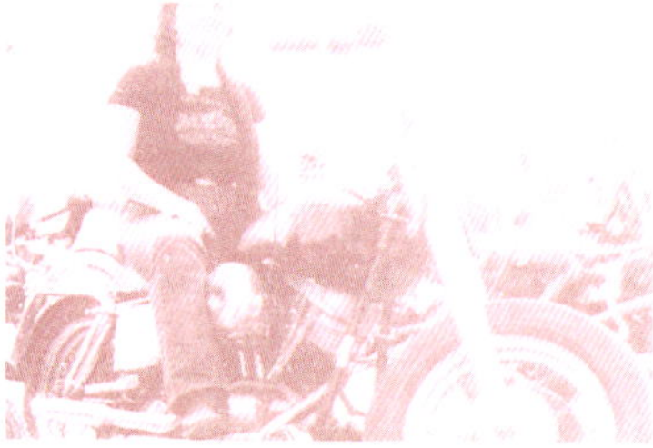

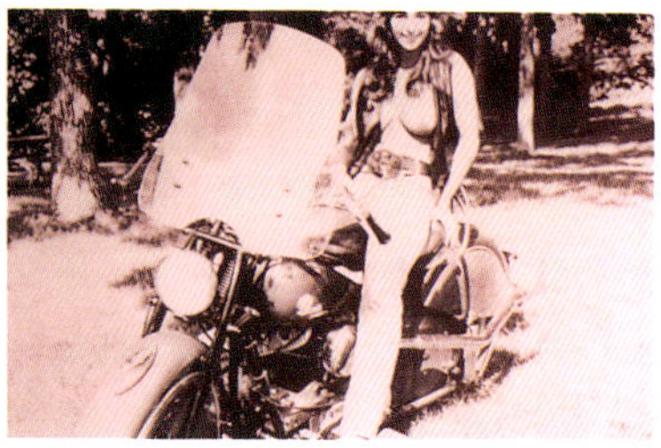

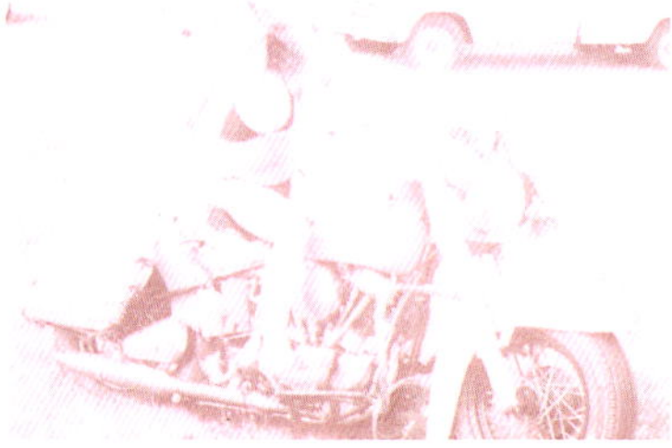

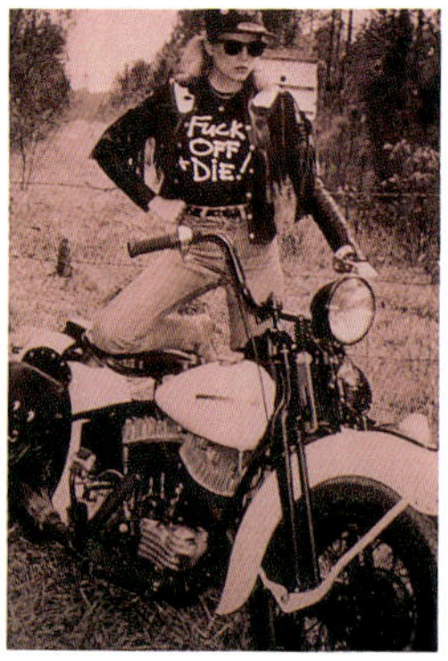
FUCK
OFF
DIE!

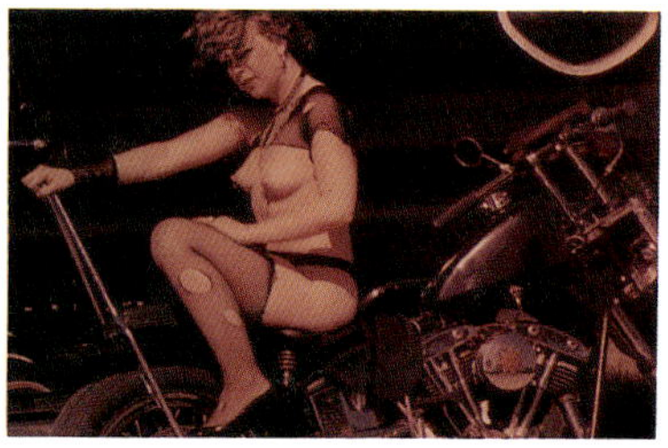

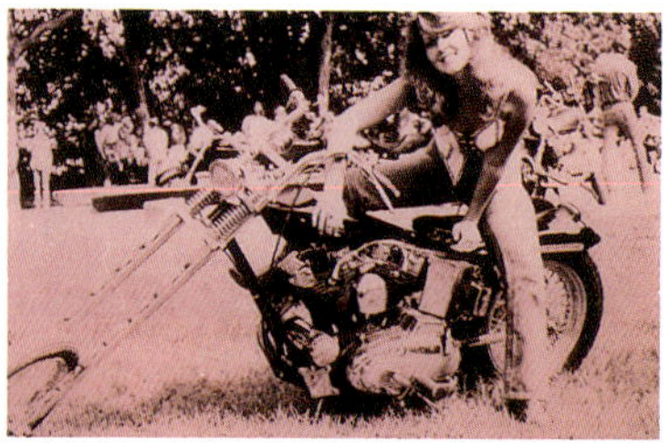

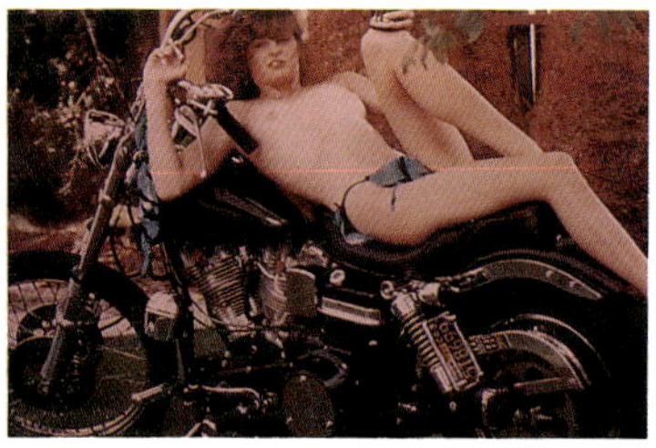

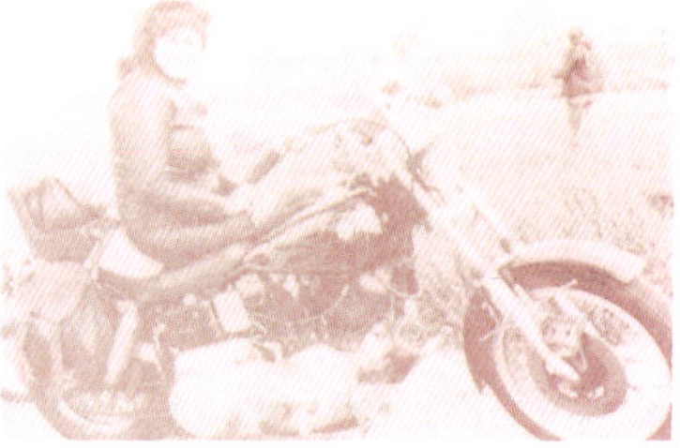

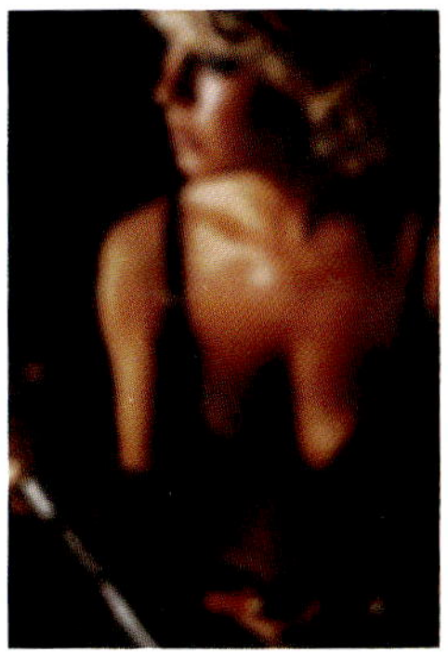
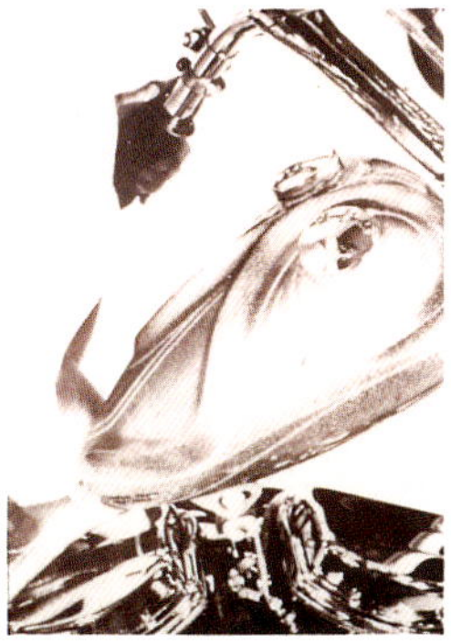
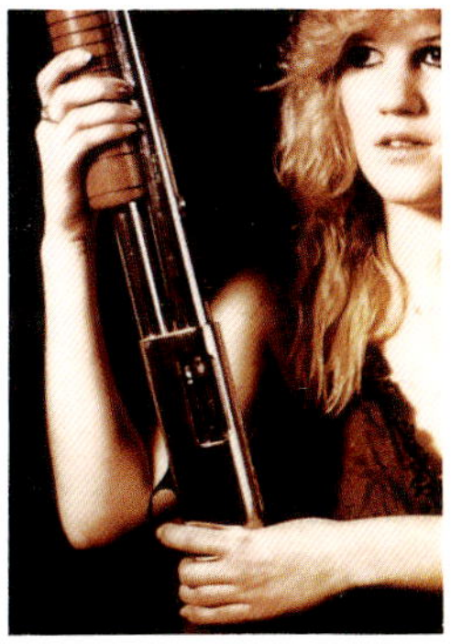
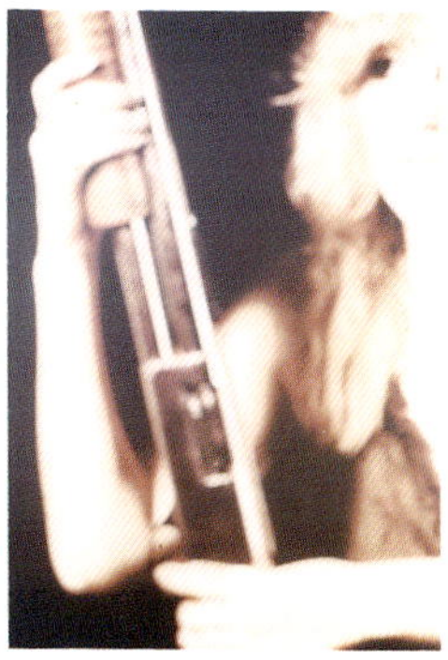
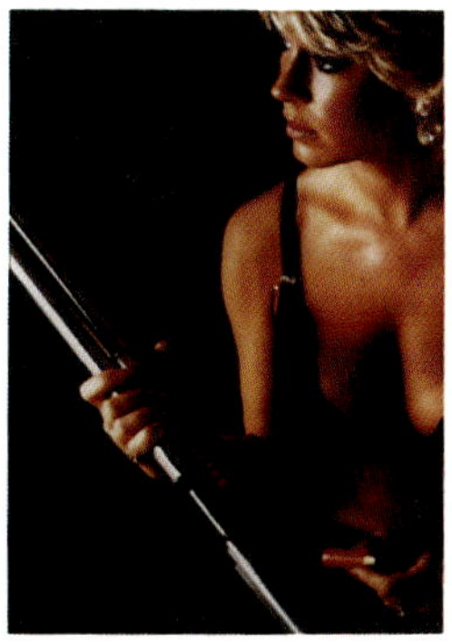
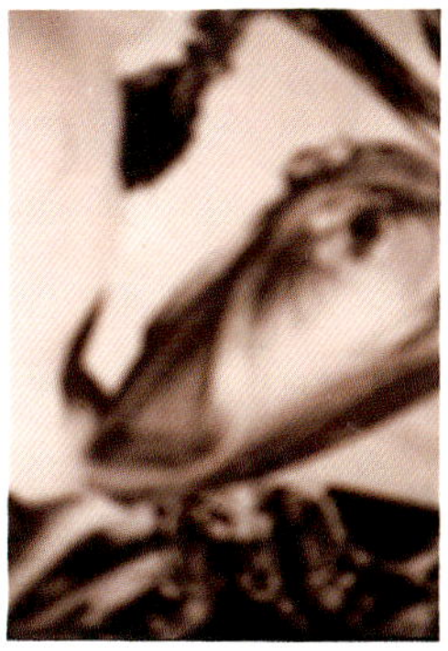
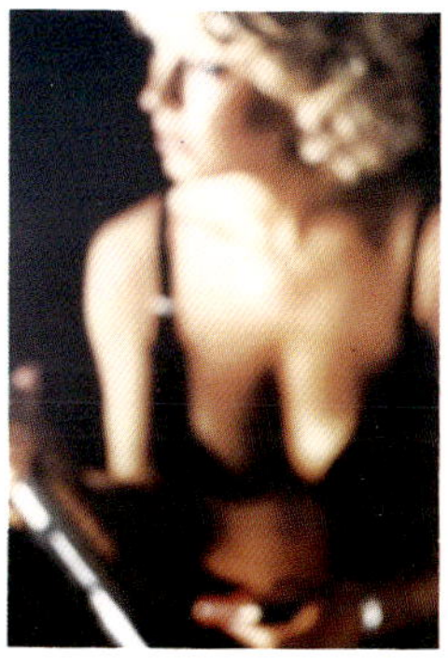
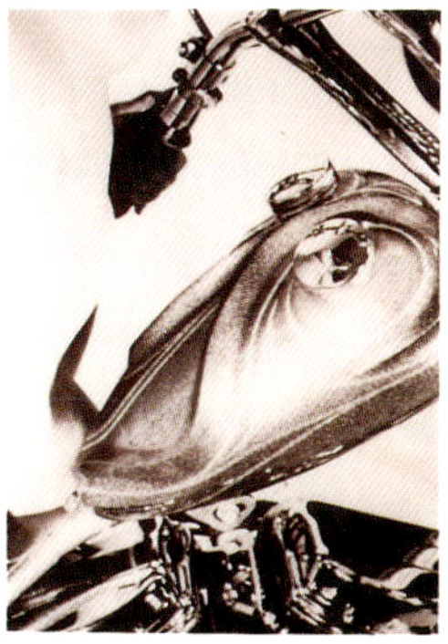
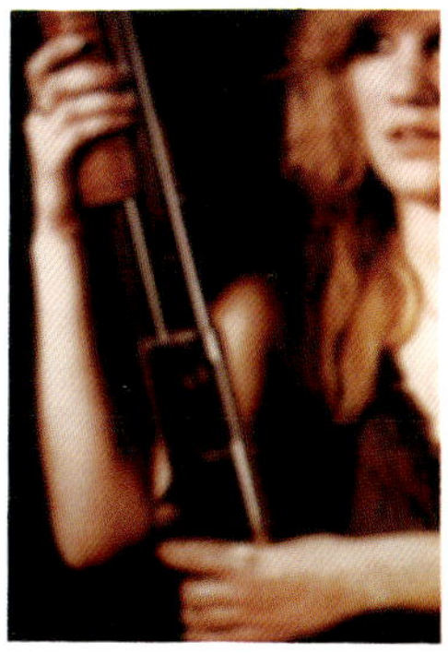

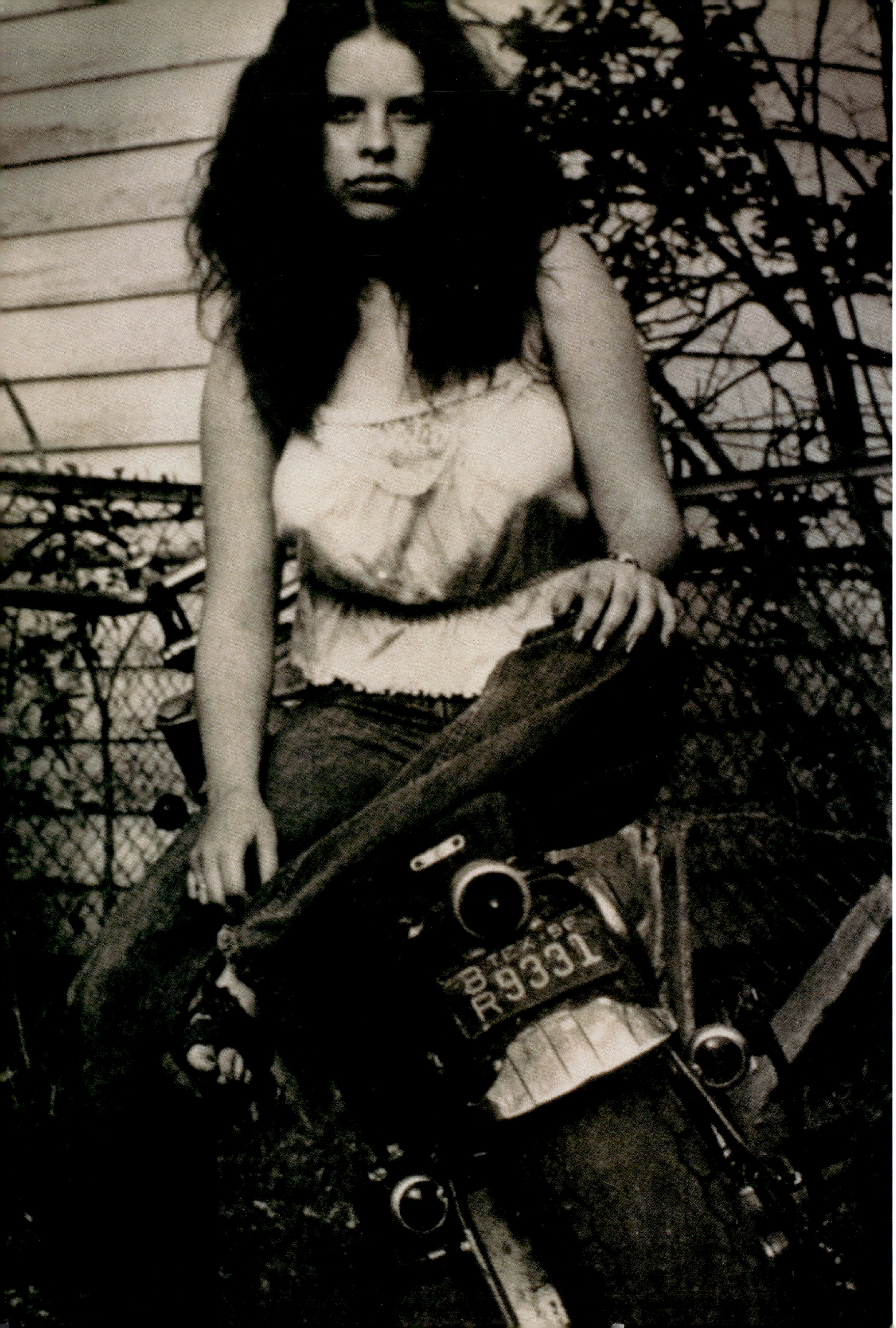
9331

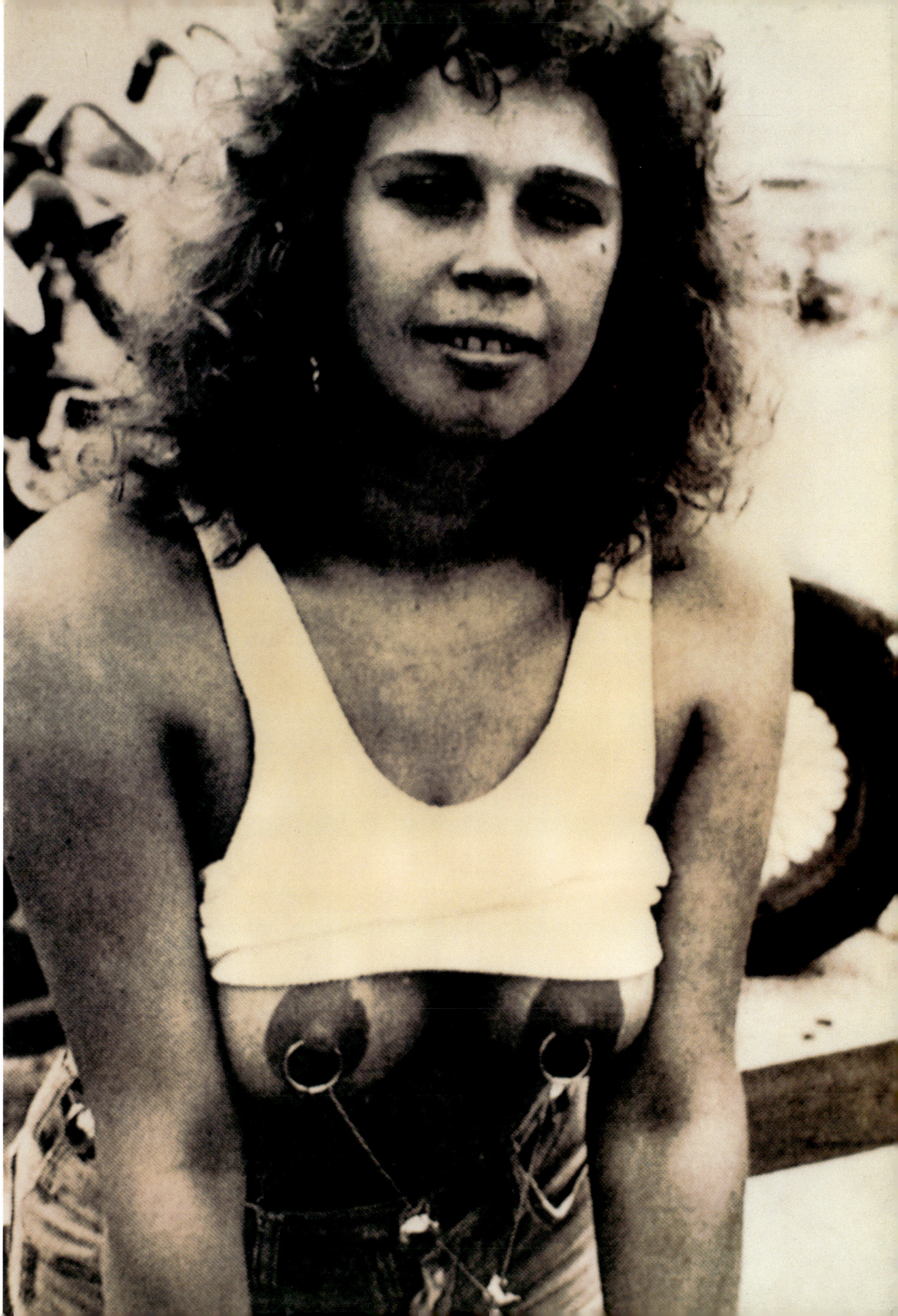

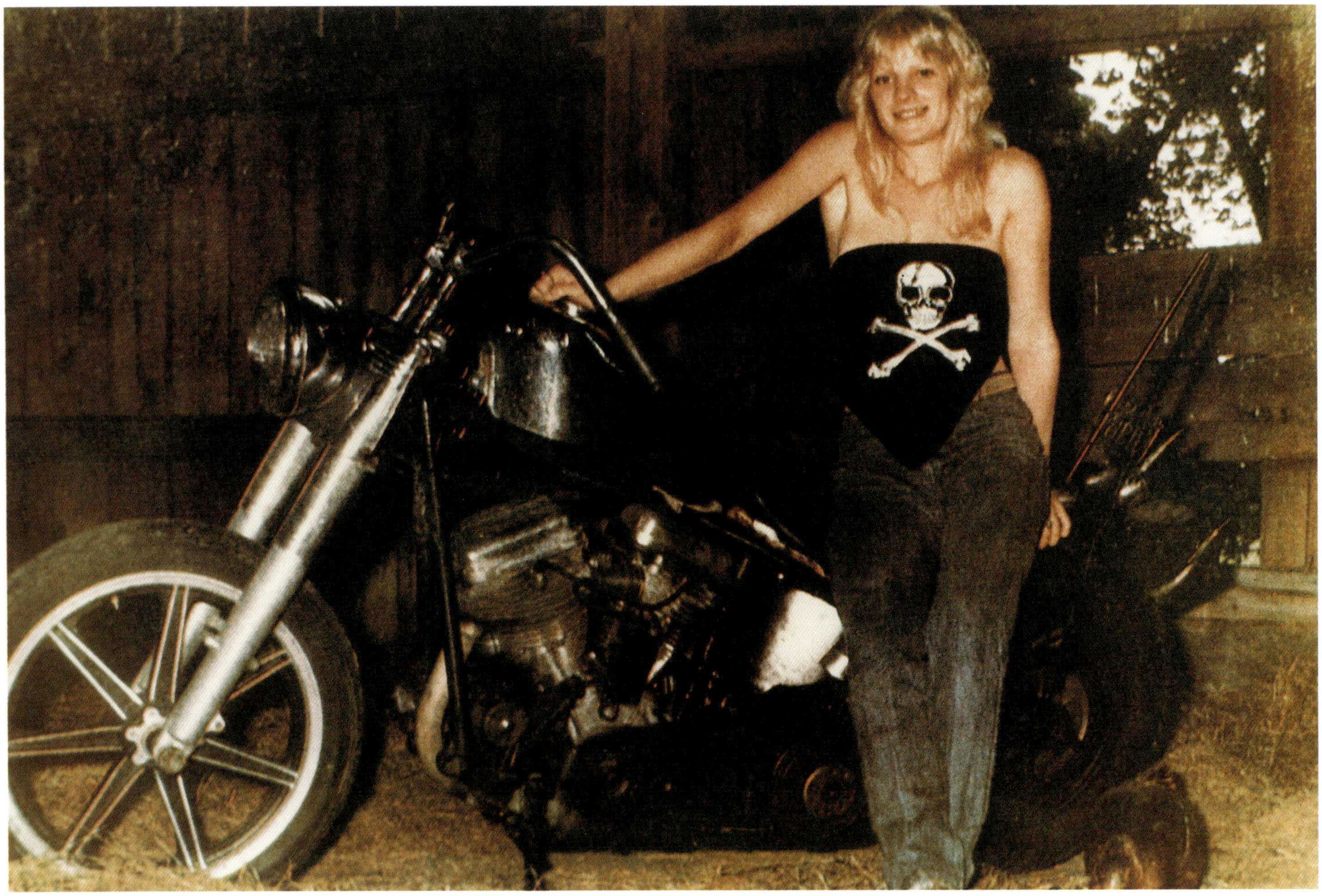

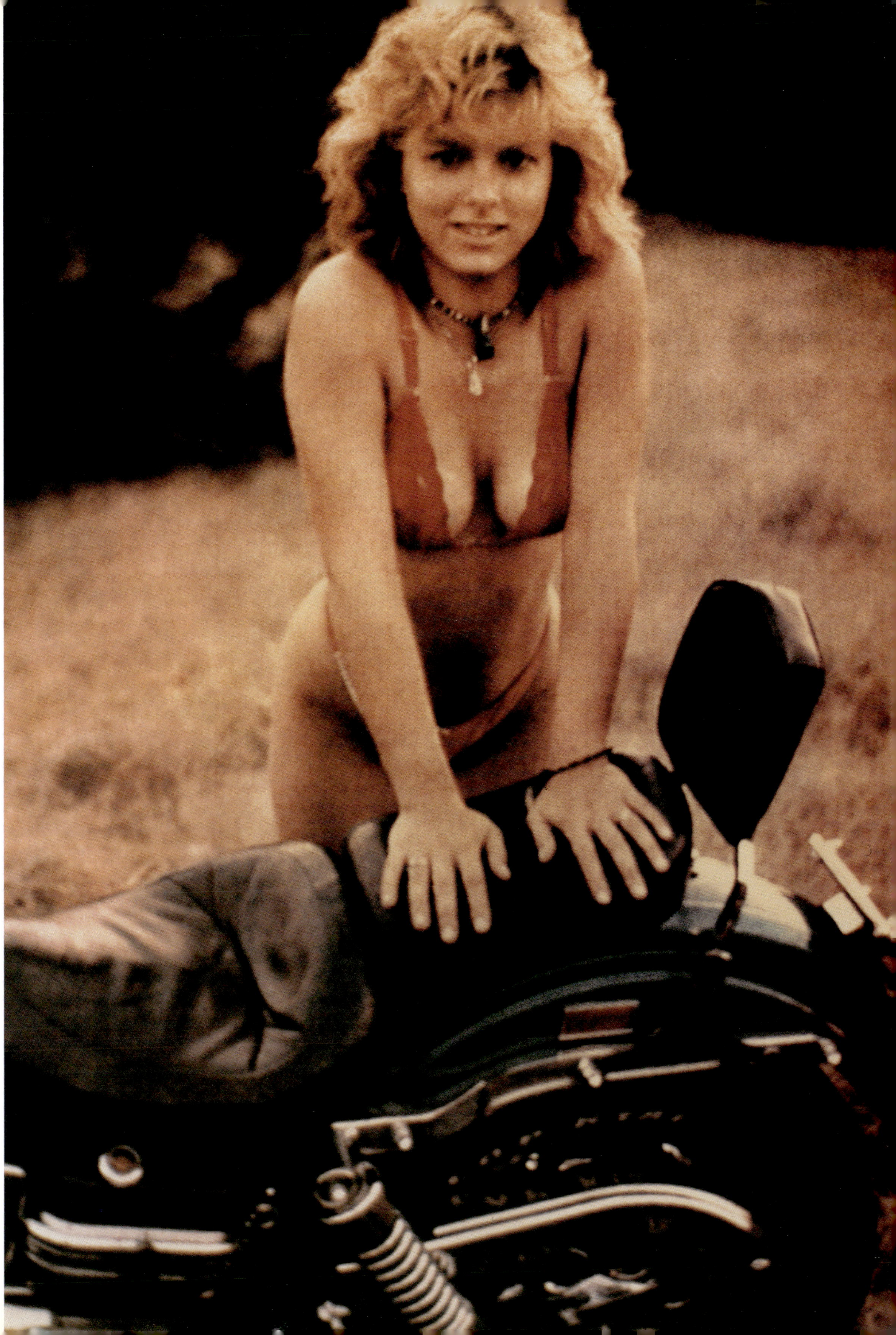

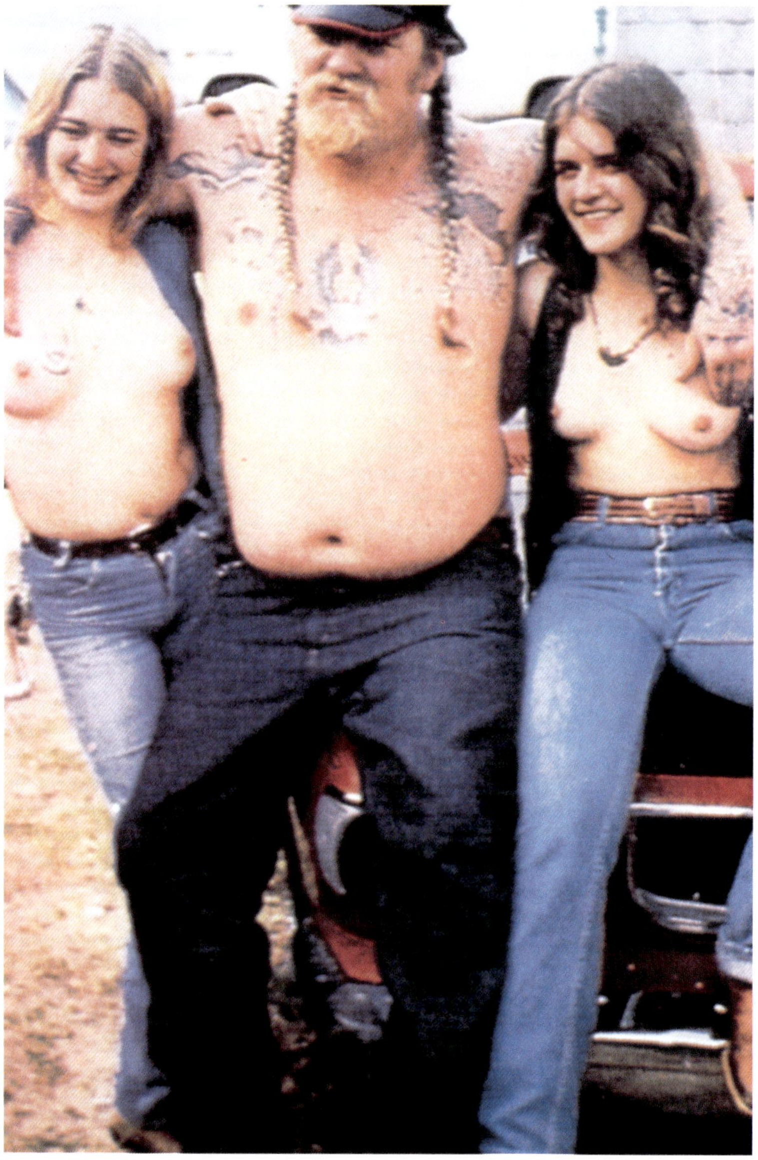

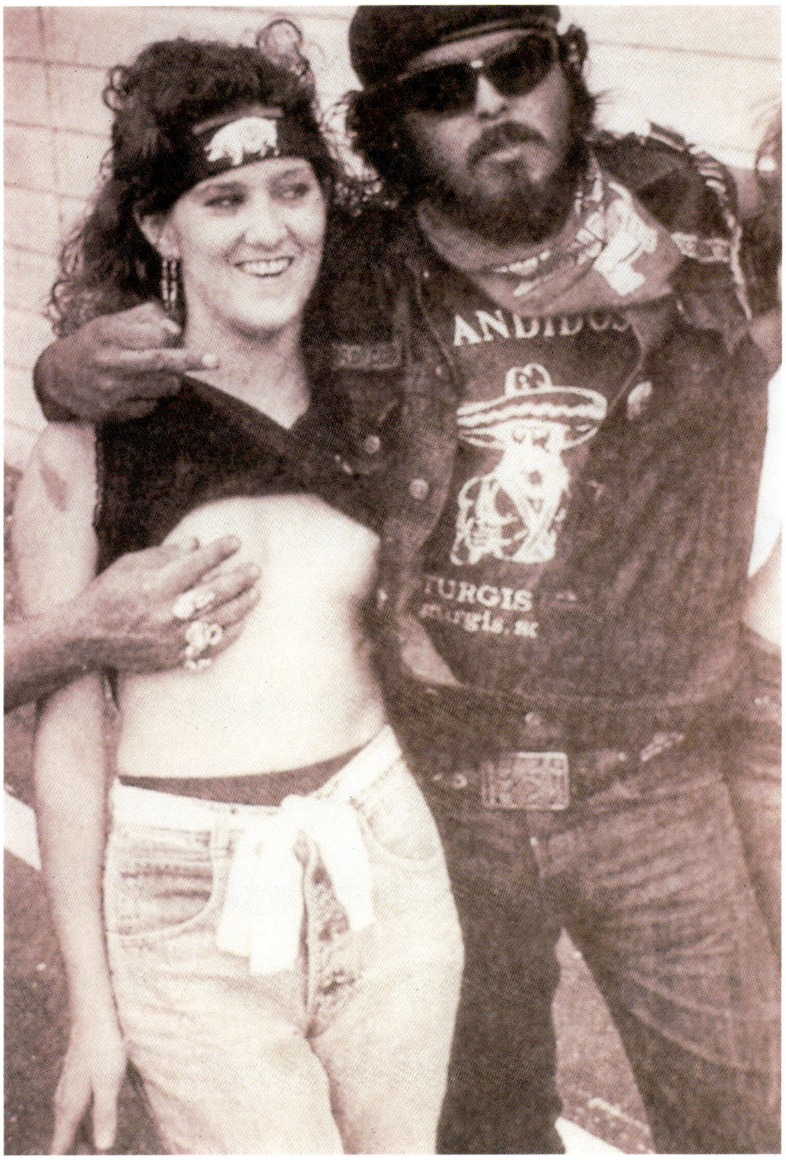
ANDIDOS
TURGIS

Nan Goldin: Sexual Outlaws

Nan Goldin's work exemplifies the themes of this exhibition: the fascination with the outlaw; the dialogue between mainstream and margin expressed in the image of the outsider; the mainstreaming of the margin and the normalizing of the *image* of the outcast through the intercession of the artist; and the celebration of community.

A local fashion supplement recently listed Goldin's successes in the art and fashion worlds: her upcoming retrospective at the Whitney Museum of American Art in 1996; her best-selling books *The Ballad of Sexual Dependency* (1986), *The Other Side* and *Vakat* (1993), *A Double Life* (with David Armstrong, 1994), *Desire by Numbers* (with the writer Klaus Kertess, 1994), and *Tokyo Love* (with Nobuyoshi Araki, 1995); the influence of her photography on the European fashion designers Miuccia Prada, Helmut Lang, and Jean Colonna; her own fashion shoot for Macy's, San Francisco; her recent photojournalism for *The New York Times Magazine*, including a behind-the-scenes look at the Paris runways.[1] To this we can add the completion of a film on her and her work with the British filmmaker Edmund Coulthard, *I'll Be Your Mirror*. She seems ideally situated for the subjects of her art to be influential.

Not surprisingly, given the fashion world's endorsement, Goldin's acclaim rests on style—her own and that of her subjects, which she has made her own. Her style approximates the unselfconsciousness of her subjects—her friends—as they go about partying, living, loving, and for some, as we know in retrospect, soon to be dying. The informality of her pictures, capturing an apparently seamless interchange between art and life, has resulted in her being criticized for merely making snapshots. But her photographs create a unique kind of scrapbook, one that is more public than personal. Goldin's initial method of presentation was to project her images back into their milieu as slide shows on the club circuit. Later to be published in 1986 as a book, *The Ballad of Sexual Dependency*, the images chronicle the "bohemian" party period of the late 1970s and 1980s in New York's Lower East Side and its axis to Berlin. Even though formalist, these works herald what could be called a neo-Beat aesthetic—the diaristic, photographic record that certain "nomadic" artists have given their day-to-day lives. These publications may be for our time the "writing" that Beat literature was for the 1950s; more than writing now, they offer us the density of lived experience of a period already past. Although that chapter is closed, part of another ongoing project, Goldin's second book, *The Other Side*, published in 1993, concentrates on drag queens, the "sexual outlaws" who are transvestites and transsexuals.

The transvestite and transsexual have been the subjects of representation before. Between 1967 and 1970, Diane Arbus, for one, photographed a number (seven appear in the Aperture monograph on her oeuvre), and they connote her fascination with the "freak"—at least according to Susan Sontag in her well-known, dismissive mid-1970s commentary: "The other world is to be found, as usual, inside this one. Avowedly interested only in photographing people who 'looked strange,' Arbus found plenty of material close to home. New York, with its drag balls and welfare hotels, was rich with freaks. . . . The photographs of deviates and real freaks do not accent their pain but, rather, their detachment and autonomy," states apprehended by the "dissociated point of view" of the artist. Only such a detachment could explain, for Sontag, the images by which this ex-fashion photographer expressed herself. "It was her way of saying fuck *Vogue*, fuck fashion, fuck what's pretty."[2]

Although Goldin was not to become a fashion photographer herself, she did want to be one. Yet even as she accepted the terms of fashion, she too was drawn to alternative subjects, but without saying fuck what's pretty. She started to photograph "the most gorgeous creatures [she'd] ever seen." It was Boston, the year was 1972, Goldin was eighteen, and they were queens. She fell in love, moved in, and for two years took pictures of her friends almost daily. "My aspiration was to be a fashion photographer; my goal was to put the queens on the cover of *Vogue*." (The latter has been accomplished, although not by her.) In 1974 she attended art school full-time, and with a knowledge of technique went back to photograph her friends. "But it didn't work: I was an outsider, it was no longer my home."[3]

Sontag's criticism of photography is based on the notion that "the camera is a kind of passport that annihilates moral boundaries and social inhibitions, freeing the photographer from any responsibility toward the people photographed. The whole point of photographing people is that you are not intervening in their lives, only visiting them." Sontag's critique does not apply to the photography of Goldin and Larry Clark. They are not visiting: these are their lives in the "extended families" they have chosen to replace the ones they were born into. For Goldin and Clark, a camera is just part of everyday life with their friends. Making *and* showing pictures became so much part of daily routine that the private moments of, say, shooting up, having sex, or masturbating hardly seem intruded on. It was through this close portrayal of community, not through photography *itself*, that each photographer became the social explorer she or he is. Goldin and Clark annihilate moral boundaries and social inhibitions because they are members of particular counter-communities as well as the artists who recorded them.

As if responding personally to Sontag's criticism, Goldin has written, "There is a popular notion that the photographer is by nature a voyeur, the last one invited to the party. But I'm not crashing; this is my party. This is my family, my history."[4] This family history details, in the words of Richard Prince, the relationships of "men and women, men and men, women and women." Those members who step out of this arena of relationships and who live on the frontiers of gender transformation, choosing transvestitism or transexuality, are the subjects of Goldin's *Other Side*: "Rather than accept gender distinction, the point is to redefine it. . . . there is a decision to live out the alternatives, even to change one's sex, which to me is the ultimate act of autonomy."[5] Ultimate acts of autonomy make an outlaw, especially when sexuality is the issue.

This book reveals two periods and two attitudes of self-presentation. The first, already mentioned, is that of queens in Boston between 1972 and 1974, and the other is a younger generation in New York in 1991 to 1992 when, like Clark, Goldin was the older one returning home. Acting from the start as "mirror" to their beauty, Goldin wanted to pay them homage. "I never saw them as men dressing as women, but as something entirely different—a third gender that made more sense than the other two."[6] The queens were still sexual outlaws, even in the gay community, when she photographed them in Boston, but by the time she took the New York photographs, they were cultural icons to their community.[7]

Although her subjects' motivation or behaviour have not changed much from one period to the next, a change in style is dramatic. From the evidence of these photographs, the late-hippie countercultural 1970s manifested a mannered stylishness more attuned to *Vogue*, but 1990s style is both a lot trashier and a lot more out there, while at the same time perhaps closer to Warhol's ideal that "drag queens are reminders that some stars still aren't like you and me."[8]

It would be presumptuous to say that representations alone can accomplish this social transformation, still by no means generally accepted. But to a large extent, artists are responsible for the images and the scenarios by which subcultures are popularized. Their own personal celebrity increases the circle of reception, and their cultural authority legitimates identification with various hitherto social outcasts.

Warhol, for instance, was his art *and* his personality, was his films *and* the Factory. After he acquired avant-garde credibility and drew attention to himself through his silent films, he consummated his fascination with Hollywood by recreating its (then) faded essence in camp parodies. These films, such as the 1965 *Harlot*, were vehicles for his own stable of celebrity superstars, and they were populated in part, in order to recreate Hollywood's mythic glamour (since "drags are ambulatory archives of ideal moviestar womanhood"[9]), by queens such as Mario Montez. "Mario only dressed up as a woman for performances—out in the world, he would never be in drag—he was more like a show business transvestite than the social-sexual phenomenon the true drags were." But "as late as '67," Warhol continues, "drag queens still weren't accepted in the mainstream freak circles,"[10] as they would be in the post-Stonewall world of Warhol's collaborative films with Paul Morrissey, which starred Candy Darling, Jackie Curtis, and Holly Woodlawn and marked a trend from glamour to trash.

"[Mark] Booth argues . . . that camp, far from being a 'fugitive sensibility,' belongs to the history of the 'self-presentation' of arriviste groups. Because of their marginality, because they lack inherited cultural capital, and thus the accredited power to fully legitimize dominant tastes, these groups parody their subordinate or uncertain social status in 'a self-mocking abdication of any pretensions to power.'"[11] Abdication, however, may take an outlaw guise, using the myths of dominant taste to promote an outcast community. If the outcast community fulfils the outlaw ideal, however ambivalently, then paradoxically it has the right to inhabit the mythic American mainstream. When Warhol silkscreened Brando from *The Wild One* or Anger stole the film's footage for *Scorpio Rising*, both seemed to be celebrating the camp, JD-looking Method actors of the previous decade rather than encouraging disobedience. Yet the inclusion of the period's symbols (Marlon Brando and James Dean) of the new problems that juvenile delinquents and hipsters posed for 1950s society, when they themselves as filmmakers were creating contemporary narratives of deviance, suggests a more calculated image of disobedience after all. Juvenile delinquency was one mask of the Factory's counter-community. (That Warhol's juvenile-delinquent film *Vinyl*, 1965, responded to the social behaviourism of Anthony Burgess's *Clockwork Orange*—the basis of the film's scenario—and that of the S/M doings at the Factory situates it among the countless experiments in new forms of behaviour and community that America has always enabled, whether they are repressive or ecstatic.)

Goldin's book, like the work of Warhol, enacts a passage between two periods of drag-queen life. But the camp artificiality and theatricality of Warhol (and Jack Smith, Queer Theatre, and others) has given way to a naturalizing of the image, insofar as this type of image, which is about masquerade, can be naturalized. Ritualizing the activities of getting ready, dressing up, going out, performing, coming home as daily routines, all of which are as well very much communal activities, also normalizes the constant gender-changing of these individuals.

Portraits of subcultures are perhaps most authentic when they are self-representations of communities by artist-members. Involvement may lessen the objectivity of the artist, but the artist is able to translate the rituals of that community into art. That it is not a record by a dispassionate observer but emerges from the lives of engaged artists assures our interest. (Could we not examine, as well, how a culture defines itself through the images it creates of the milieu of artistic practice as a species of subculture itself?) Artists draw on the full panoply of cultural influences and permissions from fashion, film, and the works of other artists that eventually gives their images themselves mythic allure. In making images, artists offer the viewer the chance to slip the anchor of identification. Such displacement of identification onto the image of the outlaw is always dangerous to society.

Notes

1 David Livingstone, "The Goldin Years," *Fashion + Design*, Winter 1995, supplement to *The Globe and Mail*, Toronto, n.p.

2 Susan Sontag, *On Photography* (New York: Farrar, Straus and Giroux, 1977), 32–45. "Most of Arbus's work lies within the Warhol aesthetic, that is, defines itself in relation to the twin poles of boringness and freakishness; but it doesn't have the Warhol Style. Arbus had neither Warhol's narcissism and genius for publicity nor the self-protective blandness with which he insulates himself from the freaky nor his sentimentality. . . . Although much of Arbus's material is the same as that depicted in, say, Warhol's *Chelsea Girls* (1966), her photographs never play with horror, milking it for laughs; they offer no opening to mockery, and no possibility of finding freaks endearing, as do the films of Warhol and Paul Morrissey."

3 Nan Goldin, *The Other Side* (New York: Scalo Publishers, 1993), 6.

4 Nan Goldin, *The Ballad of Sexual Dependency* (New York: Aperture Foundation, Inc., 1986), 6.

5 *Ballad*, 7.

6 *The Other Side*, 5.

7 Esther Newton's *Mother Camp*, an analysis of "drag queens as gay male culture 'heroes' in the mid-sixties," is a period document of attitudes on the verge of these changes. *Mother Camp: Female Impersonators in America* (Chicago: The University of Chicago Press, 1972; Phoenix Edition, 1979), xi.

8 Andy Warhol, *The Philosophy of Andy Warhol* (New York: Harcourt Brace Jovanovich, 1975), 55.

9 Warhol, 54.

10 Andy Warhol, *Popism: The Warhol '60s* (New York: Harcourt Brace Jovanovich, 1980), 223–24. "Mario Montez only 'went into costume' for theatrical roles and, being a pious Roman Catholic, worried that performing in drag was a sin. He also represented a new type of female impersonator: unlike the soignée 1950s variety, who created immaculate impressions of lacquered showgirls or campy send-ups of Bette Davis, Montez exemplified a tacky discount version of the Hollywood dream." David Bourdon, *Warhol* (New York: Harry N. Abrams, 1989), 196. That Montez came from roles in Jack Smith's films is to be expected, given Smith's underground influence, versus Warhol's avant-garde effect, especially in his film *Flaming Creatures*. For Smith and others, see Stefan Brecht, *Queer Theatre* (New York: Methuen, 1986). The drag queen and the psychopath may be the two poles of this exhibition, both consumed by an elaborate mimicry of social roles, the one sending up society's contradictions through representations, the other enacting its contradictions through violence.

11 Andrew Ross, quoting Mark Booth's *Camp*, in "Uses of Camp," David Bergman, ed., *Camp Grounds: Style and Homosexuality* (Amherst: University of Massachusetts Press, 1993), 63–64.

PAGES 52–61

Nan Goldin

David at Grove Street, Boston 1972
Ivy wearing a fall, Boston 1973
Crystal with a friend, Boston 1973
Marlene, Colette, and Naomi on the street, Boston 1973
Colette modeling in Beauty Parade, Boston 1973
Naomi under the palm tree, Boston 1973
Misty and Jimmy Paulette in a taxi, NYC 1991
Cody in the dressing room at the Boy Bar, NYC 1991

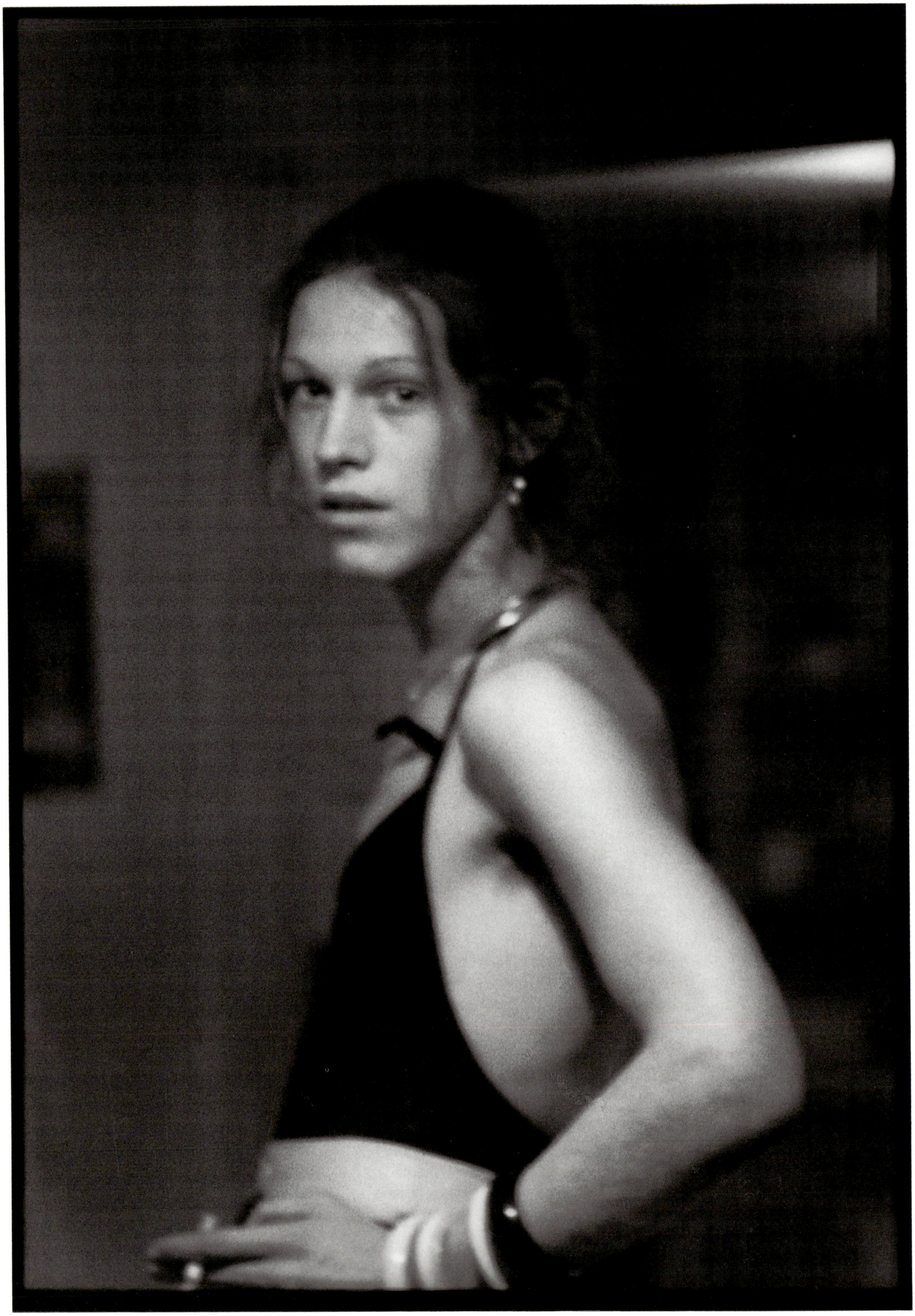

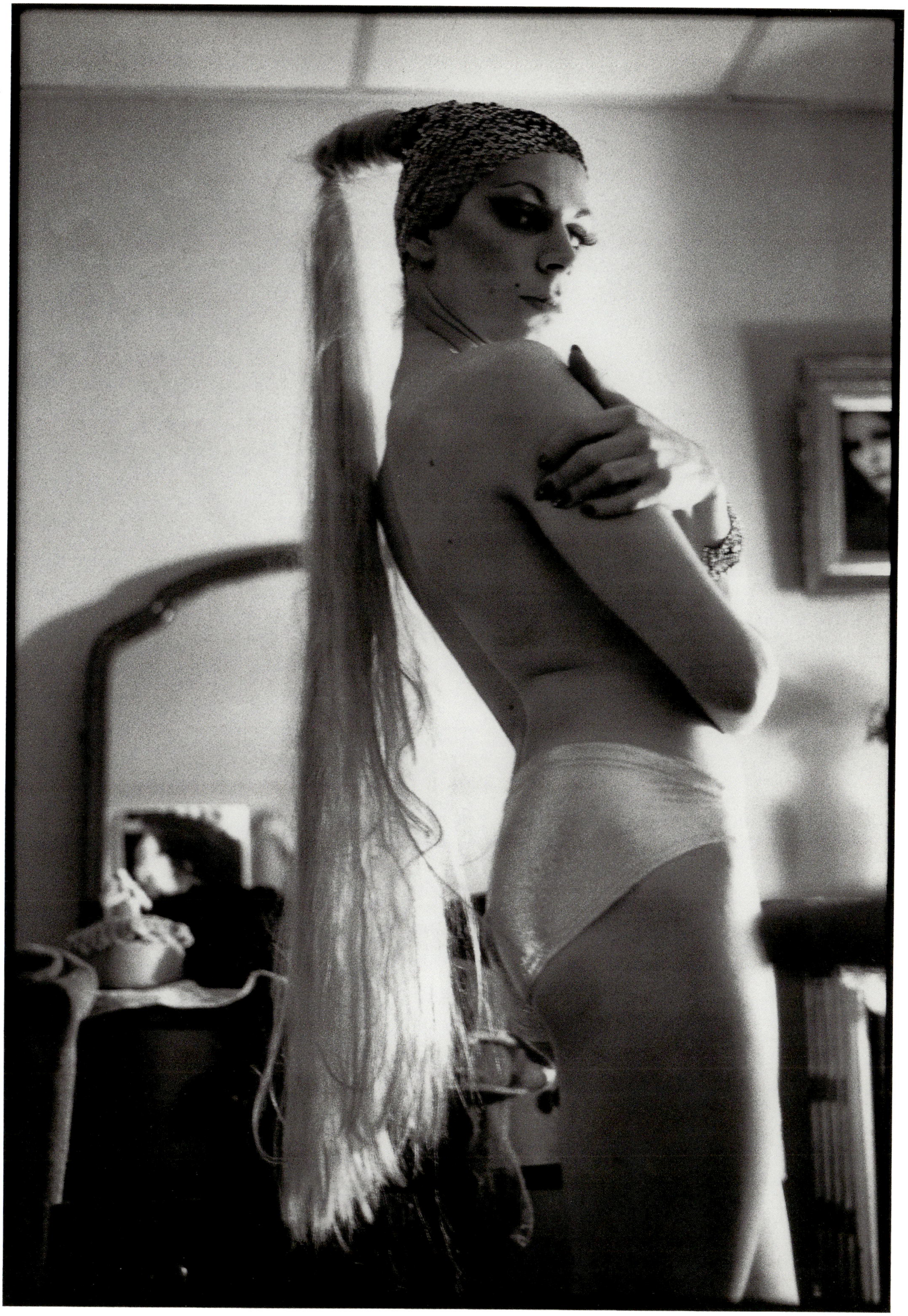

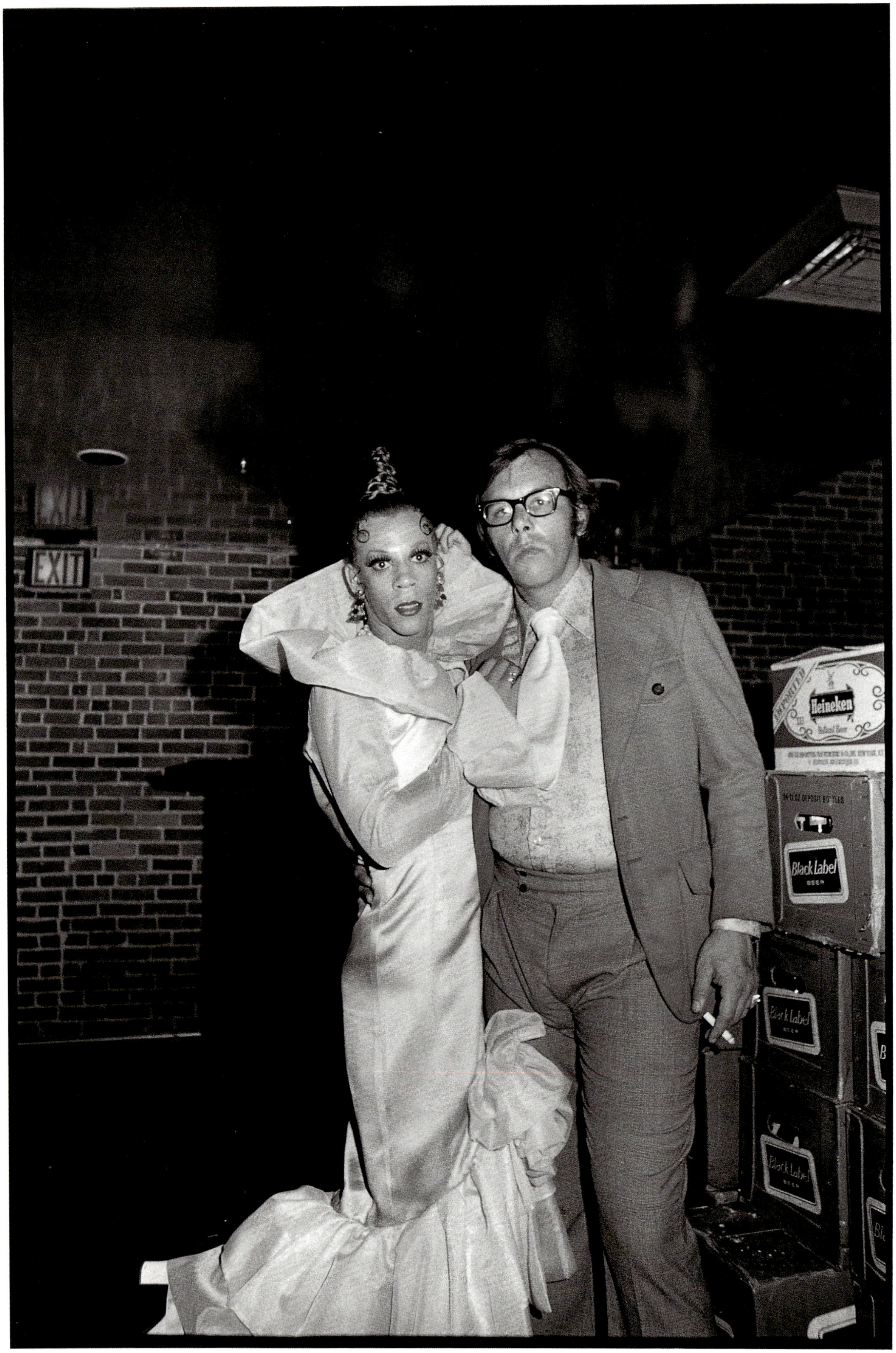
EXIT
IMPORTED
Heineken
Holland Beer
24-12 OZ. DEPOSIT BOTTLES
Black Label
BEER
Black Label
Black Label

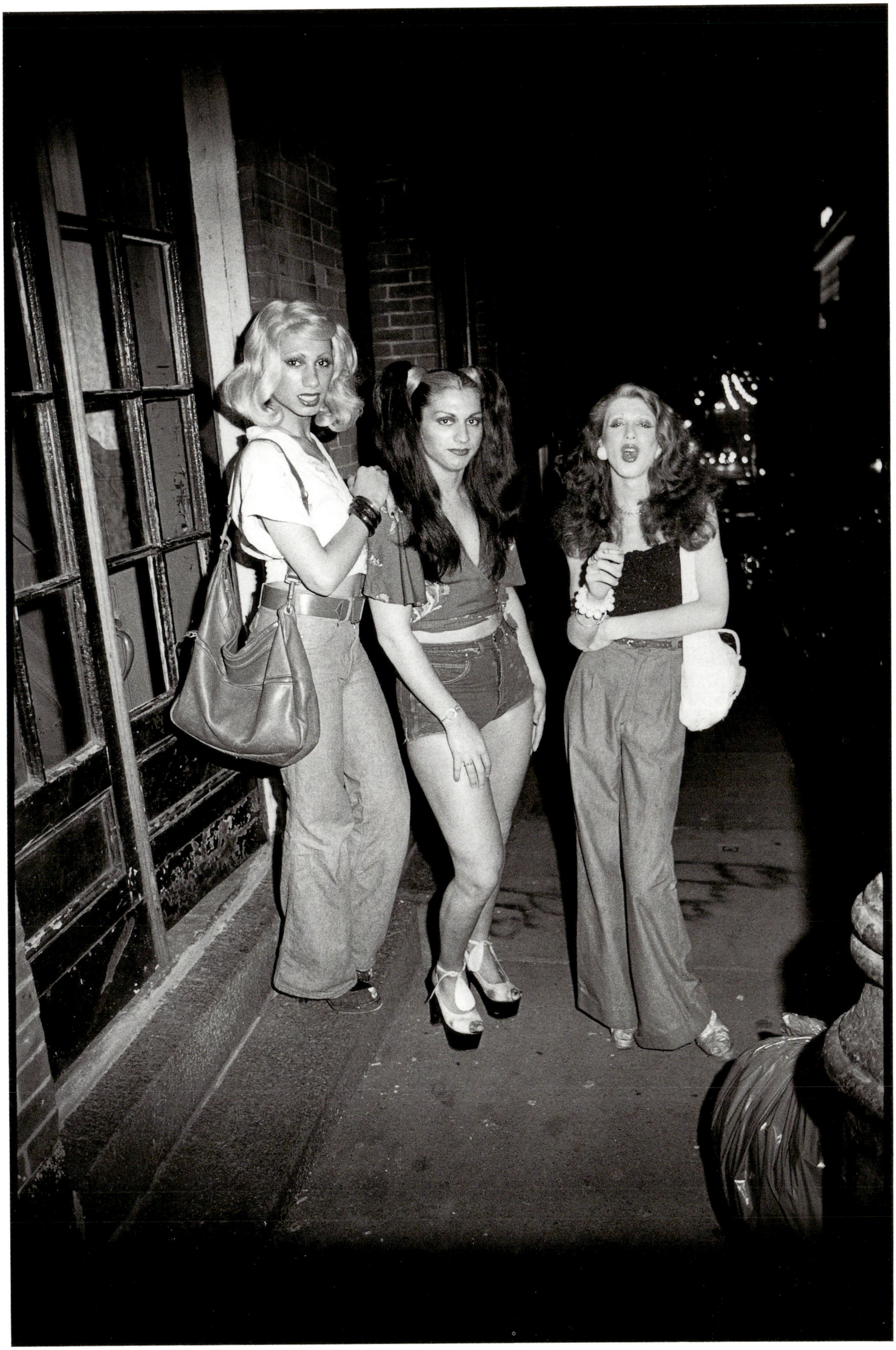

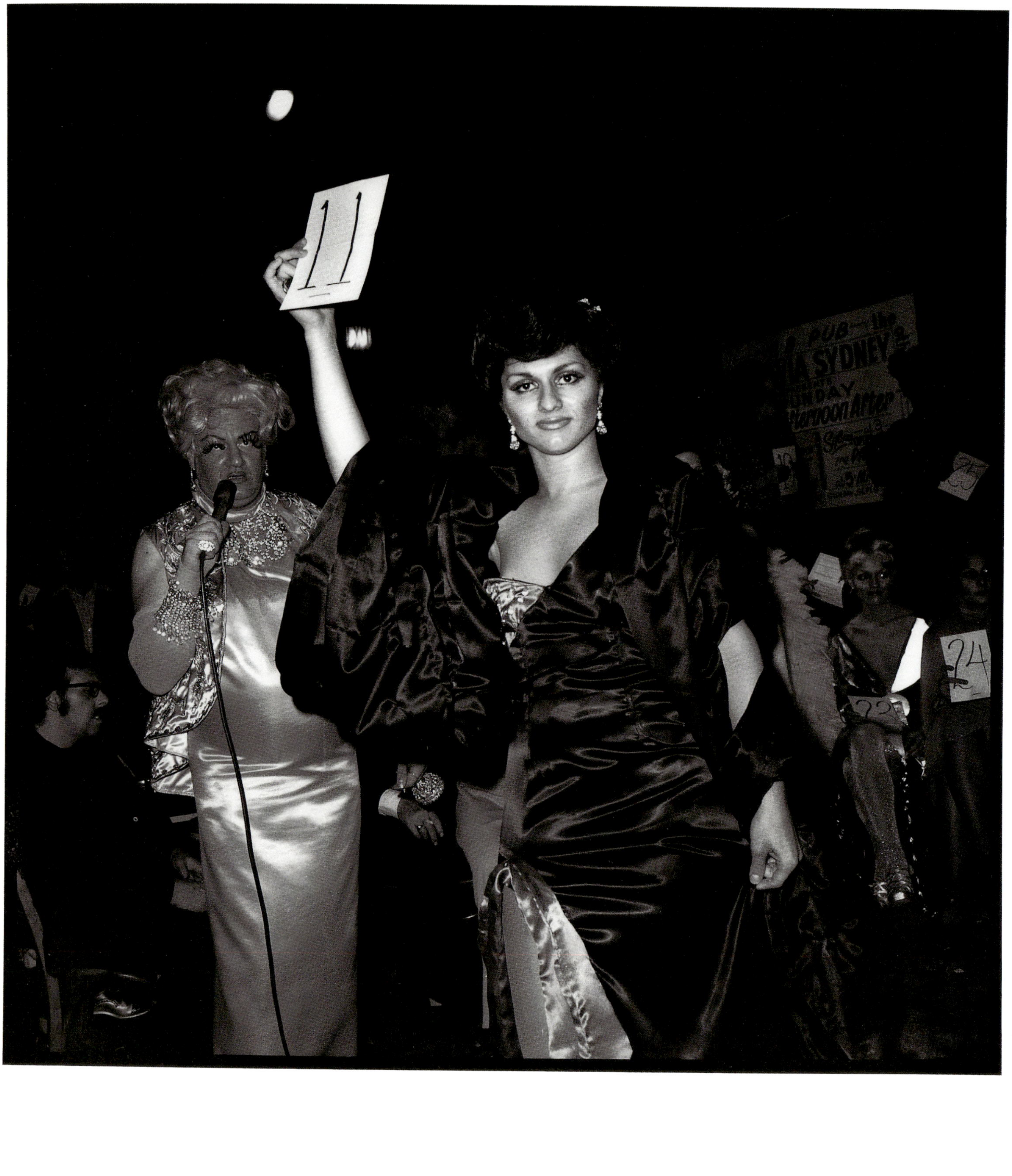
11
PUB the
SYDNEY
24
25

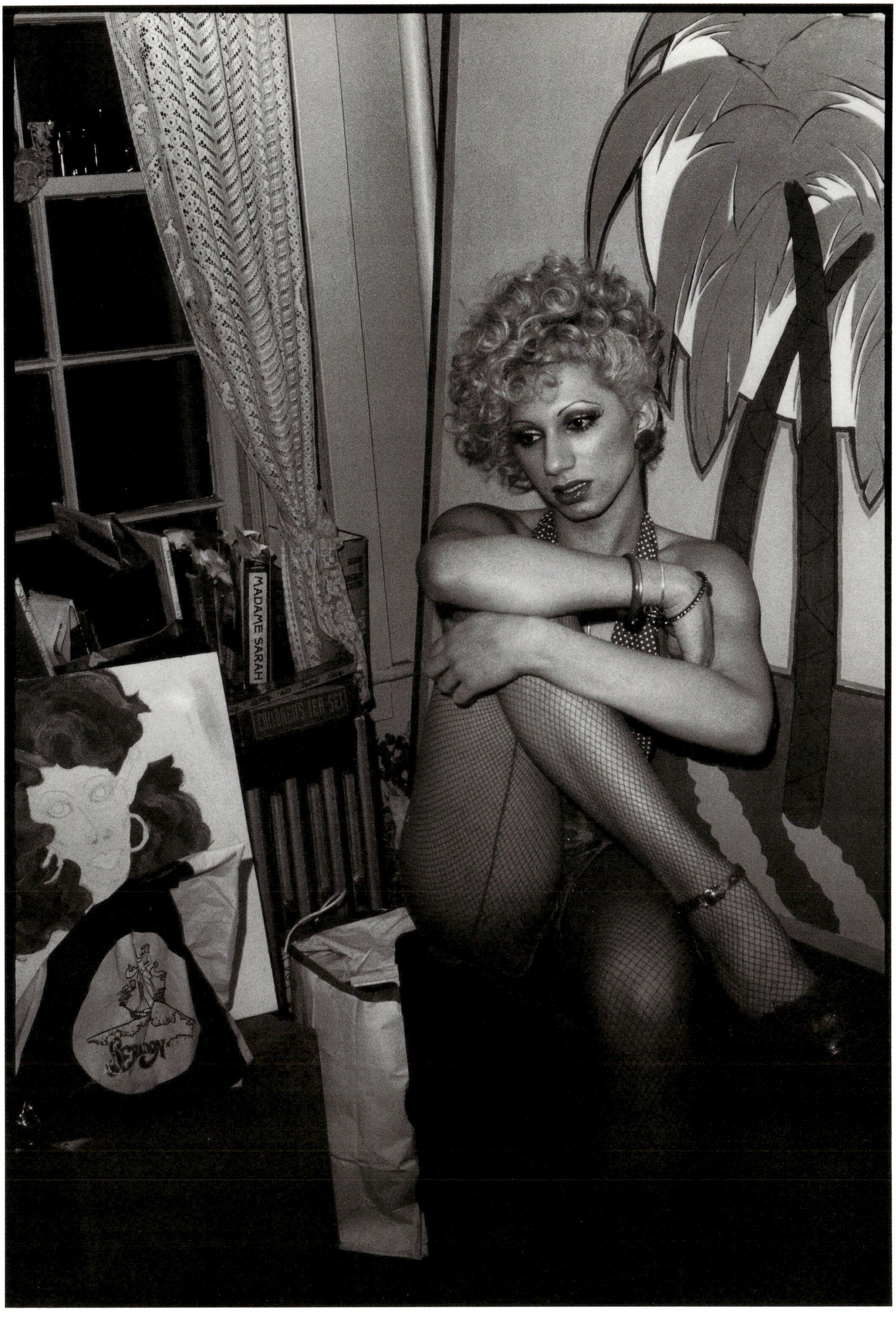
MADAME SARAH

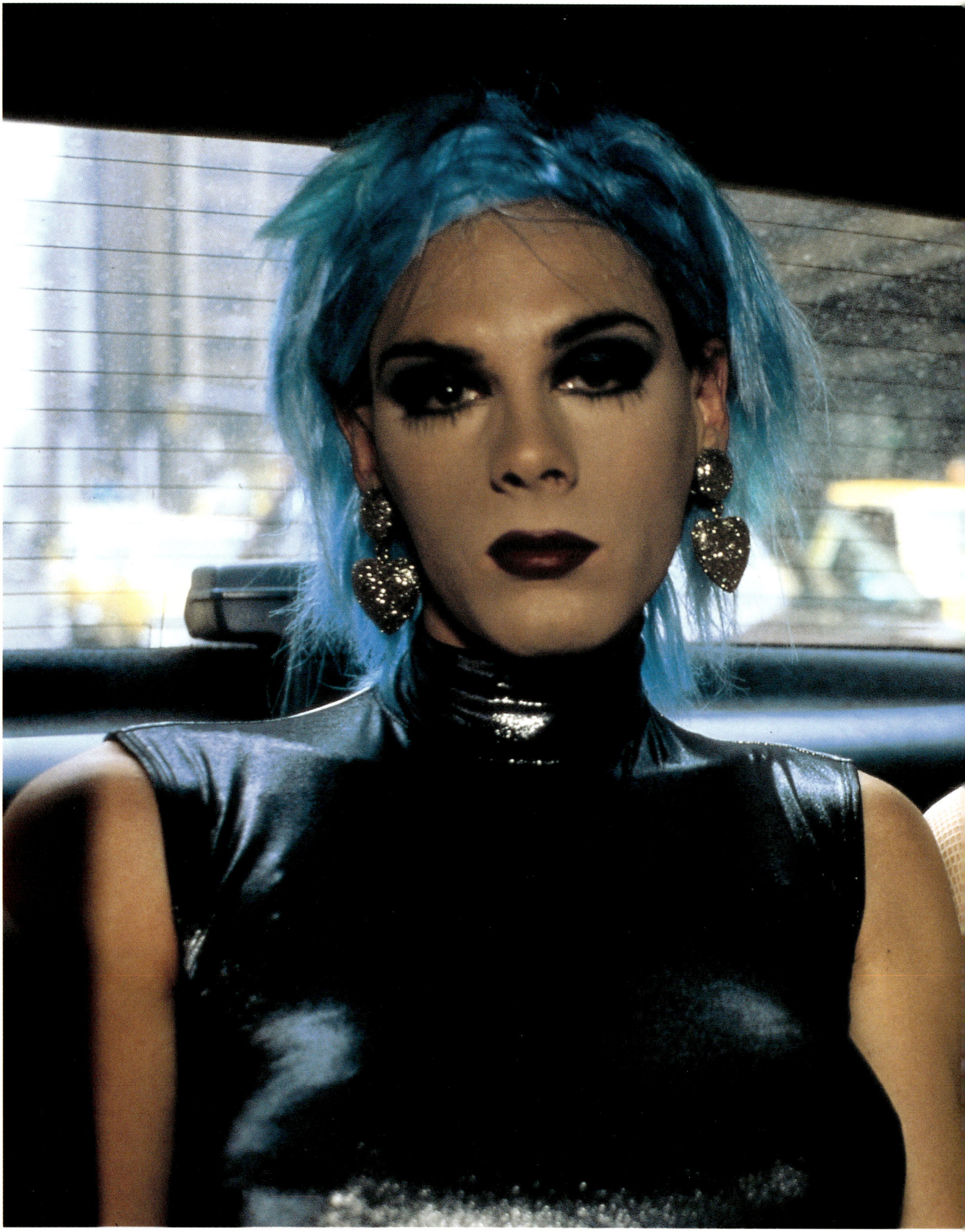

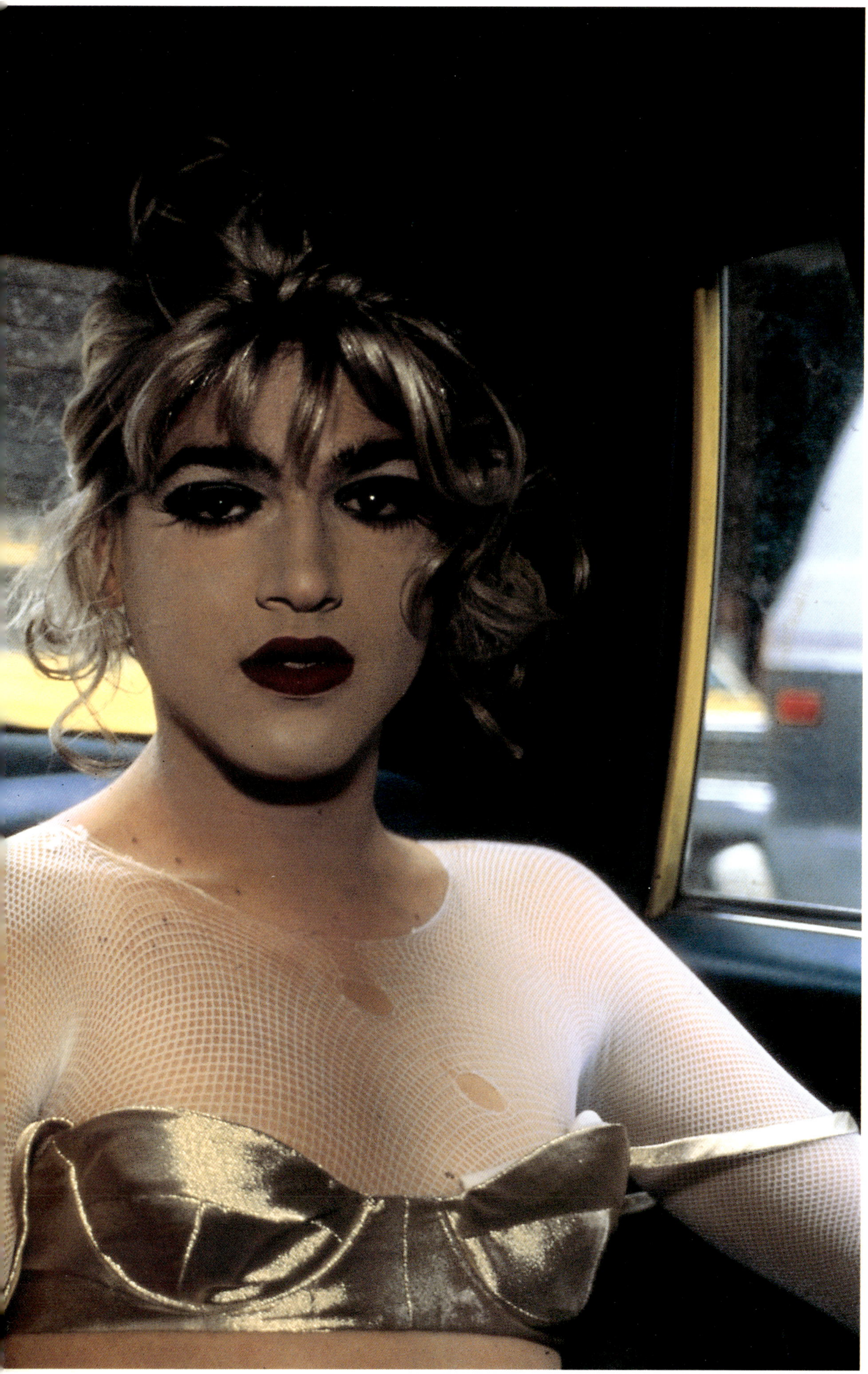

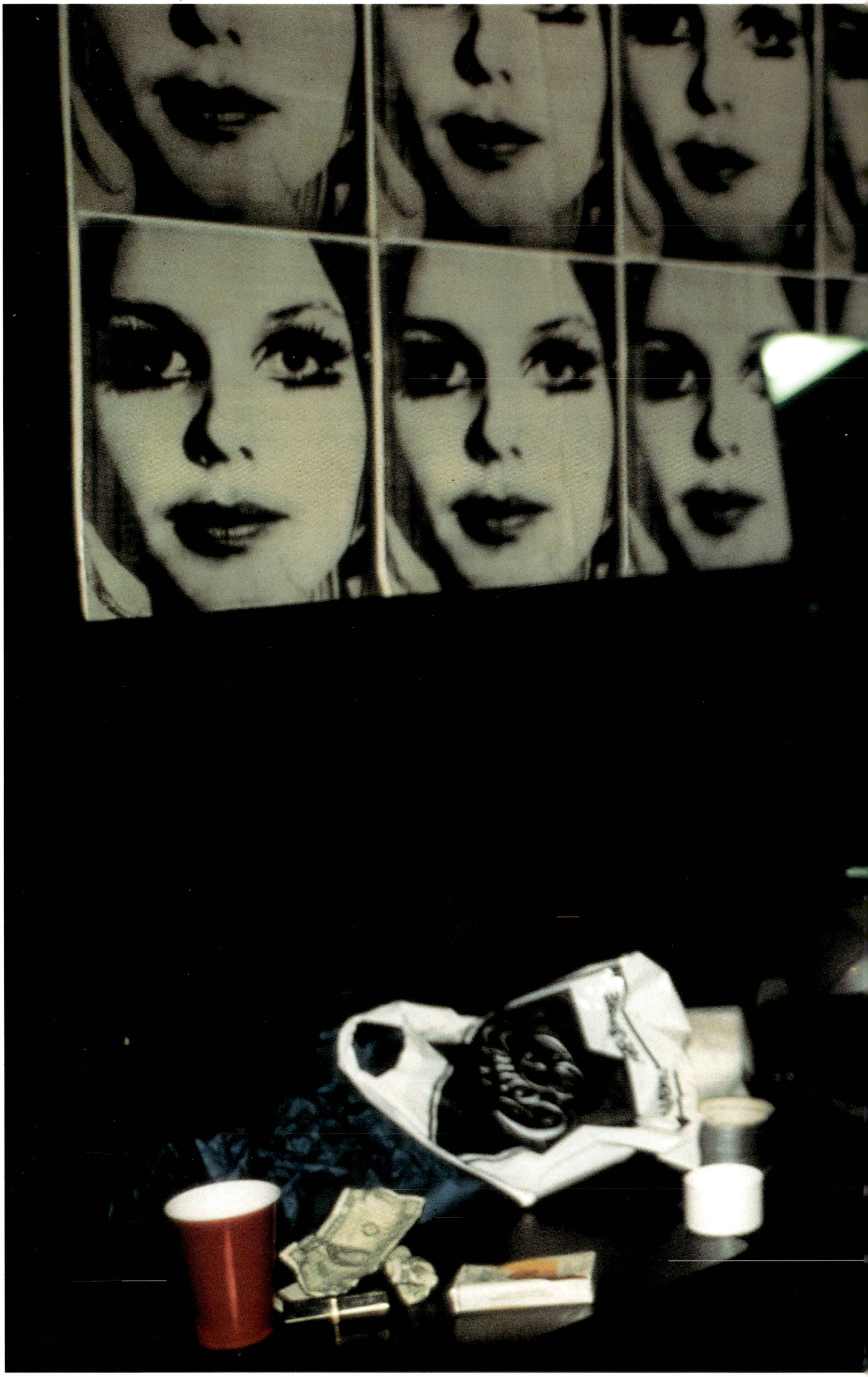

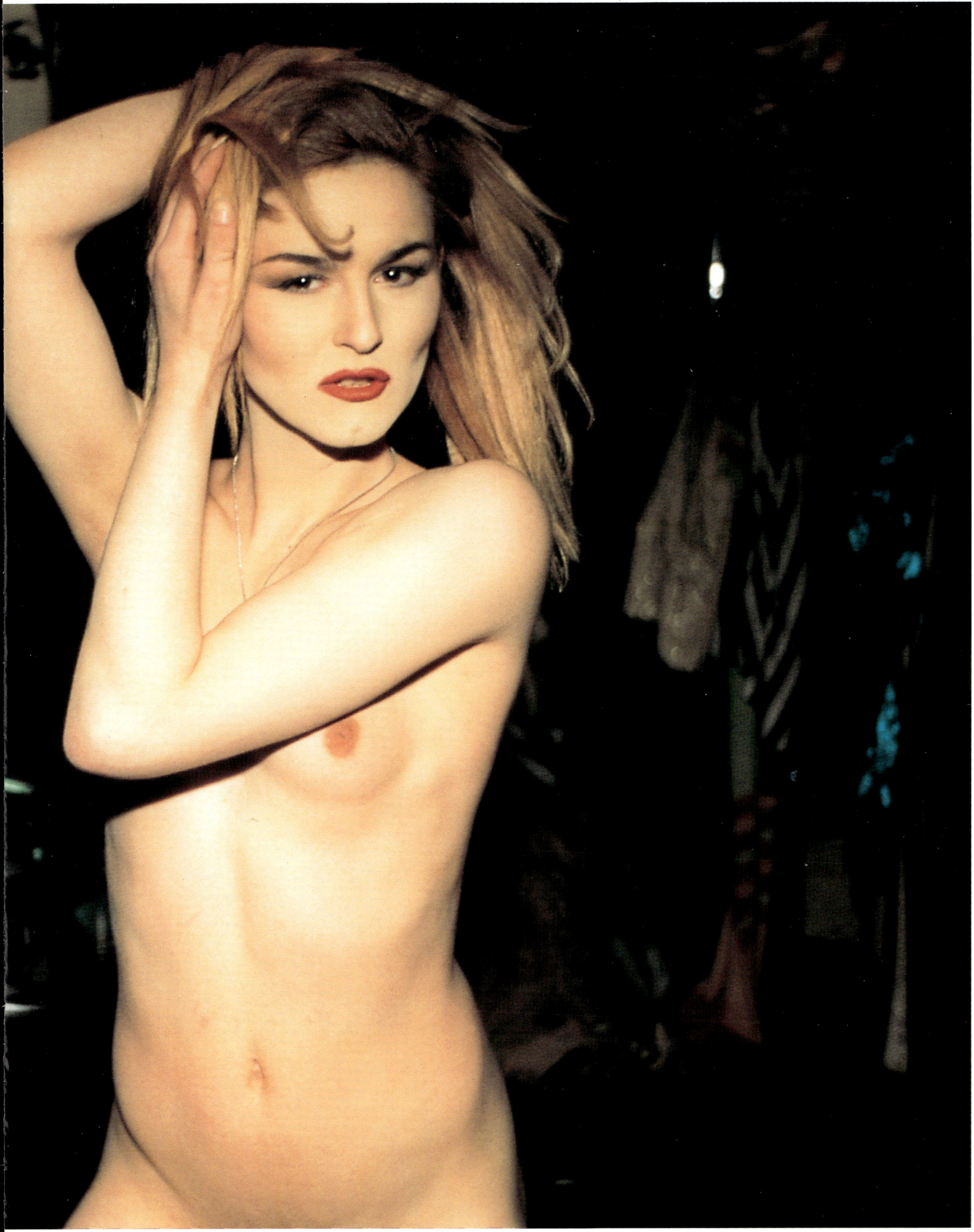

Exhibition List

Larry Clark

Tulsa 1971
gelatin silver prints, nos. 29–50
approximately 27.9 x 35.6 cm each
Gift of Benjamin Greenberg, Ottawa, 1982
Collection of the National Gallery of Canada/Musée des beaux-arts du Canada, Ottawa

"Forty-second Street Series" from *Teenage Lust* 1978–85
10 gelatin silver prints
27.9 x 35.6 cm each

Untitled 1990
laser video disc

Untitled 1991
15 gelatin silver prints from row 4
61 x 51 cm each

Untitled 1991
gelatin silver print
61 x 51 cm

Courtesy of the artist and Luhring Augustine, New York

Nan Goldin

David at Grove Street, Boston 1972

Ivy wearing a fall, Boston 1973

Colette modeling in Beauty Parade, Boston 1973

Marlene modeling in Beauty Parade, Boston 1972

Naomi and Marlene on the balcony, Boston 1972

Crystal with a friend, Boston 1973

Marlene, Colette, and Naomi on the street, Boston 1973

Ivy with Marilyn, Boston 1973

Naomi under the palm tree, Boston 1973

Roommate with teacup, Boston 1973

Marlene at home with Venus de Milo, Boston 1974

Ivy in the Boston Garden, Boston 1973
gelatin silver prints
40.6 x 50.8 cm each

Misty and Jimmy Paulette in a taxi, NYC 1991

Cody in the dressing room at the Boy Bar, NYC 1991

Jimmy Paulette and Tabboo! undressing, NYC 1991

Joey at home, NYC 1991

Joey at the Love Ball, NYC 1991
Cibachrome prints
76.2 x 101.6 cm each

Courtesy of the artist, Matthew Marks Gallery, New York, and Jane Corkin Gallery, Toronto

Cady Noland

TANYA AS A BANDIT. 1989
silkscreened ink on aluminum plate
180 x 120 x .95 cm

OOZEWALD. 1989–90
silkscreened ink on aluminum cut-out with flag
182.88 x 121.92 x .95 cm

(NOT YET TITLED). 1994
silkscreened black ink on aluminum plate
152.4 x 186.7 x 14.6 cm

BELTWAY TERROR. 1993–94
aluminum over wood
2 parts: stock, 152.4 x 142.87 x 20.32 cm; stool, 8.27 x 8.22 x 4.55 cm

BIBLE AMONG THE GARBAGE. 1993–94
silkscreened red ink on aluminum plate
182 .88 x 152.4 x 13.97 cm

UNTITLED. 1989
silkscreened ink on aluminum plate
121.92 x 182.88 x .15 cm

UNTITLED. 1989
silkscreened ink on aluminum plate
121.92 x 182.88 x .15 cm

UNTITLED. 1989
silkscreened ink on aluminum plate
121.92 x 182.88 x .15 cm

UNTITLED. 1989
silkscreened ink on aluminum plate
121.92 x 182.88 x .15 cm

Courtesy of the artist